"This astonishing memoir lives in the sacred space where life and death meet. From its first startling sentence to its last, Gelb's extraordinary story grips us and never lets go. With diamond-sharp prose, she takes us right into the shattering heart of a mother's profound love and loss. And even more, she plunges us into the universal mystery of what it is to face a life you never expected to have and, in the end, to accept with grace the precious life that is yours. In scene after vivid scene, her surprising language takes and ricochets us from heartbreak to funny, from absurd to poignant, all in the space of a few sentences. It's a magical achievement. When I reached the final page, I took a breath and began again. I wanted to experience once more the sunshine of her beloved daughter's smile, the intricacy of Gelb's relationships drawn with such wit, humor, and concision. I wanted to remain in contact with her singular voice, to revel in the wisdom she has rendered from her living, and the giant, generous heart she offers to us in this unforgettable work of art."

— Martin Moran, author of *The Tricky Part*
and *All the Rage*

"In her devastating, hilarious, pitch-perfect memoir about motherhood and mortality, Gelb proves that no family history is too tragic for laughter, no loss—even the death of a child—too painful for celebration. Filled with uncommon wisdom and hard-won insights, this book is a beacon for life's toughest moments, a welcome reminder that you're not alone. "

— Mark Matousek, author of *Lessons from an American Stoic: How En̶ ̶ ̶ ̶Your Life*

SHE MAY BE LYING DOWN
BUT SHE MAY BE VERY HAPPY

SHE MAY BE LYING DOWN
BUT SHE MAY BE VERY HAPPY

A Micro-Memoir

Jody Gelb

Kelson Books
Portland, Oregon

Published by KELSON BOOKS
2033 SE Lincoln, Portland, Oregon 97214
kelsonbooks@gmail.com

Cover by Steve Connell and Connie Gelb
Book design by Steve Connell | *steveconnell.net*

Kelson Books are printed on paper from certified sustainable
forestry practices.

Printed by Bookmobile in the United States of America

ISBN: 979-8-218-23132-3

Library of Congress Control Number: 2023941636

For Jacek and Dora
and the life we shared with Lueza

Contents

Landing in Afghanistan

Someone once compared having a disabled child to landing in a different country than originally planned. Your dreams and guidebooks were for Italy and all its treasures, and Holland, though beautiful, was not what you wanted. You had waited your whole life to see this ancient country with its art and monuments and passionate gesticulating people, and your plans were inexplicably ruined.

You were planning your life with a normal child, and your actual child was not what you expected, and life would be different. Your heart would rip open beyond what you thought was possible. The plane landed in Holland, a country that you had no interest in going to, but if you opened your eyes and accepted this new world its beauty would be revealed. I liked the analogy. It had been faxed to me by our hospital social worker when Lueza was an infant and it had become clear that she had sustained a brain injury at birth that wasn't magically disappearing, as I had hoped. The plasticity of the brain wasn't working out. A catastrophic accident had occurred. There had been a cosmic mistake. God had chosen the wrong person for this test. I was too weak to cope. Because I was so weak and hysterical, Lueza would have to be okay. This was as clear as I could figure it out. I believed in this rule. Only strong people could survive something like this. Lueza would be fine. This reasoning kept me walking and talking when I longed to drop to the floor and writhe and rend my garments.

Holland was a gentle place in my mind. I knew that they had a high percentage of home births. It was filled with Rembrandts and the sacred memory of Anne Frank. They could all speak English.

I wanted to write my version of this unexpected landing. We had not arrived in Western Europe. There were no tulips. No English was spoken. It was on the other side of the planet from where we were hoping to go. Terrorists had stolen our plane. We had crash-landed in Afghanistan. Our daughter had barely survived the landing. Her brain was exploding with seizures. Babies were dying. Mothers would arrive at the NICU and be told that their tiny premature babies would not survive. We wore yellow paper hospital robes and held Lueza, who slept for six days flooded with phenobarbital to protect her from more seizures. They gave us rocking chairs between the clear plastic isolates so I could try and nurse. She was nourished with my breast milk through a feeding tube in her nose. Her seizures became almost invisible, but then a little gray ashy color would spread around her mouth and she was seizing again. I thought Lueza was dying.

Yelling from me brought nurses who explained that it was not death. Her brain was just convulsing, and because she was so sedated with barbiturates all that showed was a lowering of oxygen in her face.

Holland couldn't be this terrifying. This was a dystopia. Birth and near death. Baby rushed into territory of hospital with other doomed babies. Giant radioactive machines being wheeled around close to babies. Babies who were see-through and not quite finished. Eyes taped shut. Sporting hand-knit volunteer-donated wool caps to maintain their body heat. Incomprehensible language being spoken. No guidebooks for Afghanistan. War unending. You could die of exposure in the frozen mountains. A terrorist could blow you up. Only way in was by warplane or a crash landing.

But the people were famous for their hospitality. They would share their last cup of tea. The beauty of the land was extreme. People lived there and raised families. The love was fierce. Someday I thought, I would write my version of Lueza's early days and how it was.

It is hard to breathe when I remember this time.

Screaming into Towels

I always wanted to be something different than what I imagined myself to be. I wanted to be a laugher with big white teeth and high insteps. To be like the ten-year-old happy blond ice-skater girl in Central Park whom my father couldn't stop talking about. To giggle with wet lips. Wet lips and big white teeth. More laughing. Less fear and nausea.

I always felt doomed. My mother was Episcopalian. My father was Jewish. My mother loved garlic. My father hated garlic. One grandmother had started life in a wealthy Episcopalian banking family and ended up living in a maid's room in my parents' apartment. The other grandmother was a daughter of a Russian Jewish kosher butcher in Brooklyn and ended up living in a French manor house. One grandmother was sweet and baked brownies. The other was vicious and wore Schiaparelli. The Jews threw fits. The Episcopalians almost never raised their voices.

Almost never.

My Episcopalian uncle had been beaten by my grandfather with a piece of lumber in the wood shed at Schroon Lake in the Adirondacks. My Episcopalian grandfather suffered from black moods. The Jews broke things. The Episcopalians retreated into their shells like turtles. The Jews made money. The Episcopalians lost everything.

I was a hybrid. Calm and hysterical. Peaceful and self-loathing. I wasn't sure what I was. Was I a beautiful child or a hideous flat-footed, gap-toothed little succubus? If only I had read the Buddhists earlier and realized that I didn't have to believe my thoughts. But I did believe my thoughts. When I was nineteen and locked myself in my childhood pre-war bathroom and got the thought of taking a razor blade out of its container and slashing my left thumb, I did it. In 1975, when I thought about killing myself at Boston University because I would never be the Greatest Actress in the World So Why Bother Living, I didn't want to do it but I didn't question the thought. Never wondered why a self-assassinating entity lived in my brain. I just slashed my thumb or the underbelly of my left arm when the melancholia overwhelmed me. Stuck my face into the towels in my bathroom and screamed like an animal. I faced the mirror and watched my face contort as I wept. I secretly hoped that someone would notice, but, because I was orderly about it and always hid the little dried scabby scars, nobody noticed and nobody rescued me from my killer thoughts. You could have the thought and then punish yourself for having the thought and then feel sorry for yourself for the thought about the thought and the unending doom. This is probably why people like heroin. You can finally rest from your mind. I would never take heroin, but at fourteen I locked myself in my mother's bathroom closet and searched for prescription medication and sleeping potions. Darvon, an opiate for the low hot pain of menstruation. Barbiturates for relaxation. It was never too many pills. Never too many slashings. I didn't have an addict inside. I had no interest in dying. I wanted to be rescued.

Who would save me? Would anyone notice? But life remained orderly. I went to drama school. Wrote the papers. Read the plays. Memorized the monologues. I remember reading and falling in love with a play about a severely disabled epileptic and speechless child in a wheelchair. I remember leaping and rolling across floors in hope of theatrical transcendence. Admired my grayish-yellow forearm bruises from forward rolls on linoleum as we flung our bodies through the air like Grotowski-style Polish theater artists. The actor as instrument. I understood none of it. I drank beer and tequila in blues bars and spied on the women around me who looked comfortable being alive. I loved an overconfident actor with short wide feet, hairless legs, and a deep admiration for marijuana and Charlie Parker.

I remember the endless afternoons sleeping my senior year. The visceral deathy feeling of my self-doubt—or was it self-loathing? Dry-mouth nausea.

Cutting the underside of my left forearm somewhere in this apartment with a piece of broken glass. Small cuts that I could hide. It was never a problem.

What do people remember about me from college?

You're Not Tits and Ass, but You're Not an Ugly Comedienne, Either

—You're not tits and ass, but you're not an ugly comedienne, either.

The head of the talent agency was holding his thumb and pointer finger in a little circle and looking through it. An imaginary camera lens. What kinds of parts would I be right for? How could I make money for the agency? Which box would I fit in? Not pretty enough for the pretty parts, and not ugly enough for the uglies. I needed to have a look. I felt like the blind men trying to describe the elephant, and I was the elephant and the blind men. I had no idea what I looked like. I didn't know what my colors were. And I didn't like being stared at.

Thoughts on Stage Fright

Imagine everyone in the audience sitting on toilets. Imagine everyone in the audience naked. Picture the audience covered in dust. Imagine greeting your mentors from the past. Take drugs. Breathe like a Navy SEAL. Stop being so narcissistic. Squeeze a pressure point between your thumb and forefinger. Jam your finger into a spot on your front ribcage. Tap your meridians as you accept your fear. Surrender to the riptide of terror. Float. Eat bananas. Take thumbnail and dig deep into flesh of opposite hand. Do deep squats offstage before entering. Pray to Jesus and Quan Yin. Curse the audience. Confess your dread to a kind-faced stagehand and clutch his hand. Get a prescription for beta-blockers. Quit the business.

He Could Whistle Puccini

I married my husband because he could whistle Puccini. I met Marek in Warsaw in 1988 when I arrived with six actors and three stage managers from Actors Theatre of Louisville to perform short American plays and monologues for Polish people. I was thirty-two. It was the year before the Berlin Wall would come down.

I had always wanted to travel to Poland. A place of intense artistic expression and dark unfathomable gloom. I had read Michener's *Poland* after getting the job offer. I studied my Berlitz phrase book and learned how to pronounce words with *szcz* and *prz*. I learned that they drank tea in glasses with beet sugar and that men still kissed women's hands.

The plays were performed in English. Marek was one of three live translators/interpreters seated in a small room near the stage. The audience wore tiny earphones. We met in a hallway at the Palace of Culture and Science. Introductions were made between the American actors and Polish interpreters. His smile. Something in its complete openness went straight into my brain, where I made the split-second unconscious judgments that he was kind and empathetic and loved children. Two days later, during a rehearsal, he offered me a sip of his orange soda and asked me to see a Polish play with him that night. We started at a Warsaw café that served nothing but hot chocolate in green china cups. We went to a theater and watched a Polish comedy, and he sat next to me holding my hand and whispering the translation into my left ear. My hand was inside his long fingers. The muscle tone was soft. Large hands. Big well-shaped feet. After the play, we wandered around a late March, rainy Warsaw and he kissed me under a tree branch and whistled a Puccini aria. I can't remember which aria. Probably "Un Bel Di" from *Madame Butterfly*. Doomed love. He had kind man hands. I knew that I could survive the death of my mother with this man. My parents would love him. I would get acting jobs. He would translate. We would read the *New York Times* in bed. Children would be born. They would run down the hall and leap into our bed. Running and leaping children. Wild joy. We would inhale their skin. I would become normal.

The Banishment of the Polack

I had been summoned to my parents' apartment. My childhood home. Next to the Guggenheim Museum, where we roller-skated on the smooth Fifth Avenue pavement and bought Good Humor ice-cream bars from the possible pedophile. I was told to get rid of this new Polish boyfriend. This possible spy. A nothing of a human. A silly foreigner. A ridiculous man, who might wear cheap sad suits. Get rid of him or risk a shunning as sharp as disinheritance. I might as well have been an Orthodox Jew marrying the village Polack. I eyed the knives embedded in the butcher block and plotted a split-second slashing of my inner forearm. Grab long knife with right hand and slash inside of soft underbelly of left arm. That would stun my father. Shut him down. And they would think I was crazy. So.

No slashing. Just more screaming down the long carpeted hall hung with family photographs and into the living room and falling onto the rug in front of the fireplace.

—Just dump him.

My father explained how fun it could be to drop

someone for no apparent reason.

—If I owned a chocolate store, what you did wouldn't matter.

I had recently been selling truffles in a Madison Avenue Swiss chocolate shop. An out-of-work actor job. But there was talk of a significant political appointment in 1989, and it wouldn't work if he had a daughter with a Polish spy living in her apartment.

—Get rid of him.

My mother was there, but I can't remember if she spoke or agreed or just looked sad. My mother. The love of my life. She was usually silent when the screaming started in our home. Pulled her arms and legs in and hid in her turtle shell. Her life with this high-strung family of screamers. At some point, I said I would get rid of the Pole. He would disappear. I would figure it out. And then they drove me back across Central Park to where this Polish man was waiting for his beloved, who had inexplicably left him alone the day after he flew to the U.S.A. to join her.

We moved into my best friend's empty apartment five blocks away. I told my father he was gone. The Polish national had left. A few weeks later we moved back into my apartment and Marek filed papers to become a permanent resident alien. He signed documents stating that he had never been a member of the Nazi Party or committed a crime of moral turpitude. We brought the love letters and photos to prove that it wasn't a green card–seeking fraudulent marriage.

Ten months after the banishment we sat down to pancakes in my parents' kitchen, and my father was happy and talkative, asking Marek questions about Polish history and the destruction of Warsaw during the Second World War, even though Marek was born nine years after the Nazis dynamited most of the city. My father sang the Polish song he had learned from his best friend in the Navy, a Polish American who had taught my father about the Poles saving Vienna from the Turks, and we were all so happy. When my grandmother met him three weeks later, there was a short exchange.

—You are Jody's greatest tragedy. When are you going back to Poland?

Marek leaned forward and kissed her hand.

—Jody has told me so much about you. It is a great pleasure to finally meet.

Two months later we married in my parents' living room in front of the fireplace as he stood in black plastic shoes. I dressed in my childhood bedroom. I walked down the hallway to Bach's *Jesu, Joy of Man's Desiring*. My parents looked happy. I cried during my vows. It was two days before Christmas. Two days before the execution of the Ceausescus in Romania. I had a bad feeling about those plastic shoes, but he refused to wear the leather Oxfords that I had run out to buy at Harry's Shoes on Broadway two hours before the wedding. For some reason we were doomed.

Who's Tommy?

I am doing eight shows a week of *The Who's Tommy* at the St. James Theatre on Broadway. Our cast is getting invited to dinner parties by Pete Townshend. The Who. The guitar-smashers of the rock era. We're hanging out with *Pete* at the Royalton. *Pete* is our friend. At thirty-seven, I am the oldest woman in the company. We're invited to parties with clothing designers. I'm in the ensemble and have eight costume and wig changes in the first ten minutes of the show. I'm a minister's wife, a nurse, a whore, a doctor's assistant, a secretary, and a policewoman. My first Broadway show as an original company member. My name will be on the cast album.

I understand the role of Mrs. Walker, the accidental adulteress and mother of Tommy, an emotionally traumatized boy who becomes deaf, dumb, and blind, and then a pinball wizard. The morning in late August when our Upper West Side building is struck by lightning is the same day that the lead actress phones me to say that she is leaving the show because of trauma to her vocal cords. I am terrified, but I am ready, thanks to Friday understudy rehearsals and a supply of beta-blockers that will control the overflow of adrenaline and stage terror. As Mrs. Walker, I watch Tommy be fed through a giant brain-scanning machine as we search for the cause of his sudden loss of sight and hearing. I try to imagine the suffering (or is it terror?) of this mother five months before I will become pregnant with Lueza.

The Madness of a Cuckquean

My shrieking was scaring him. A thirty-seven-year-old childless woman married for three and a half years realizing that I was what? An unlovable shrew? A melancholic with hysteria?

This was probably when the neighbors woke up. We were familiar with the screaming from the Hasidic Jews across the hall. Once, I found Lybush sitting on the doormat outside their apartment when Rachel had locked him out during one of their fights.

Now the screaming was me. I grabbed the Swiss cowbell Marek had brought me from the layover in Geneva on the way home from his work in a Central Asian republic that I had never heard of. Tried to crush it. Mangled it. Bloodied my cuticles. Ran six steps to the living room in our apartment. Opened the window to West Eighty-Sixth Street and flung out two dozen pink peonies that he had brought me when he got home from the business trip with economists and interpreters.

Was I stuffing my knuckles between my teeth? Was I making guttural sounds? He started crying.

Six hours later I was on a bus heading from the

St. James Theatre to Radio City Music Hall for our
Tony Awards rehearsal. *The Who's Tommy* was up for
eleven Tony awards and we were about to win five. I
was live on television in a white 1940s nurse costume
seventeen hours after crushing the Swiss cowbell.

She was Irish and going through a divorce. She
had large wet Irish eyes. We were supposed to be
happily married, but it was something else. Existential
depression was hanging over me. Over him. A feeling
of dread. Incompatibility. Claustrophobia.

I called information for the international organization in Washington D.C. and was transferred to her
office.

—This is Marek's wife.

—Oh. I'm terribly terribly sorry.

—Please tell me that you won't see him again.

I hear my breath. My tongue is drying out.

—I'd like to tell you that I won't be seein' him,
but I can't tell you that. I can't tell you I won't be
seein' him. (heavy Irish accent)

I feel like vomiting may happen. I am now Medea
without children.

I craved revenge. I imagined traveling to her office in
Washington D.C. with a metal bucket that I would fill
with rotten milk and cheese and pour over her head as
she tried to enter her building. I imagined I imagined
I imagined.

And Marek could not help me because he could

not speak about it. Not speaking about it was mental torture for me, and speaking about it was mental torture for him, so we stopped trying. I had eight shows a week to do. The theater was like medicine. And besides, my parents told us about their affairs and that nothing could break them up. This was fate.

I had no more saliva in my mouth. Breathing was like panting. I could only eat once a day. I couldn't sleep. I told my story to a doctor to get sleeping pills. My mother dropped off an envelope of yellow tranquilizers wrapped in toilet paper with the Polish doorman who looked like Lech Wałęsa. I spoke to an Egyptian taxi driver about my marriage. He said this would never happen in his country. He was nonplussed.

I started writing haiku.

Irish women were everywhere. Black eyelashes and pinkish freckled skin. Enormous sad eyes. I gave away my Enya albums. Sinéad O'Connor enraged me. I hit my thighs so hard I had small pink palm prints like tattoos.

I went to his bookshelves looking for Irish books. There was a new shiny little book of Irish poetry. She had written something to Marek inside the cover. I took it to the back hallway, where the building garbage cans lived. It was small and easy to rip in half. I found a book of Yeats and slipped it into my bag for the subway trip to a Saatchi & Saatchi commercial audition. I tell myself I will not destroy another book. I will find a stranger who loves Irish poetry. I spot him leaving the subway. We're both heading to the Saatchi building. He's on my elevator.

—Excuse me, but do you like Yeats?

—I love Yeats.

—Here. I need to give this to you. My husband is in love with an Irish woman.

—Thanks. Stop by my office after your audition if you want.

He's a small man with a kind face. He shows me a video of a breakfast cereal commercial that he wrote. He tells me to leave my husband. There's no hope, he says.

On the subway ride home after my audition I imagine scenes of love and sex. Flailing legs and tongues. Piles of weeping wives left behind. The shrewish wives who have lost their husbands to the joy of sex with northern Celts.

Ireland and Poland. Catholics and suffering and potatoes.

I want his plane to crash and to live my life with dogs.

Winter

I got pregnant on a frozen Monday night, January 2, 1994, in North Stamford near the Merritt Parkway in Connecticut. My grandparents had bought this house in 1939. Now the place was empty in winter. Marek and I started coming up on Sundays after my eight-show week with *Tommy*. I knew it was a good day to get pregnant. It had been seven months since I had removed all Irish books from our apartment. I had given the ring back for a few weeks, but I knew that we were supposed to have our children.

Turbulence

—The baby is not happy where she is right now.

The doctor said it very calmly, like an airline pilot when things start to get scary. They probably sound calm even when the plane is crashing. We were crashing. We were all about to smash into tiny pieces.

I had imagined a natural birth with the music of Hildegard von Bingen playing quietly on the boombox that my husband carried to the hospital. I had always looked forward to birth. Always wondered about the pain of labor. How bad was it really? I read the books written by hippie midwives who refused to call it pain and instead called it "rushes." I asked questions of my friends who had labored without drugs. What kind of pain was it? Was it screaming pain? Was it the kind of pain that made you cry? I wanted to know. I wanted to experience it. I wanted to labor bravely without medication. I wanted the catharsis of birth. What had women been going through all those millennia before there were drugs? Was it like Hollywood depictions of birth? I always cried when I saw those scenes. The sweating woman with matted hair shrieking as she pushed out the baby. I had once watched the birth of a horse in France. Cocktails in hand, we were silent as the mare lay on her side with the shiny white birth sack hanging from her horse private parts. The farmer was murmuring in French to the mare and holding the emerging front legs of the foal until she slid out in a whoosh of liquid. The mare let out a sigh and then stood up with the torn placenta swinging from her until it dropped onto the hay. We watched for another ten minutes as the mare nibbled on the soft rubbery hooves of the foal. Nobody wanted to speak. The clinking sound from ice in the whiskey and sodas seemed intrusive. I held a glass of silent red wine. There was a roaring sound in my ears. Like my head was in a giant seashell. Finally someone decided that it was time to go back to the house and eat dinner and we mumbled our *mercis* to the farmer and his wife and quietly left the stall.

My favorite documentary about childbirth featured a famous French obstetrician who embraced his birthing mothers as they stood with their arms over his shoulders and delivered their babies. I remembered one of the French women saying "for-mee-dah-bluh" (formidable) over and over as her baby emerged into the arms of the father. My other favorite documentary featured an endless sequence of babies being born from squatting women in Guatemala. It was shot in black and white without sound, so if there was any screaming it was not recorded.

By modern hospital standards my daughter's

birth had been going quite well. When I had gotten to the hospital that afternoon after a whole night of contractions in our bed, the doctor had convinced me that labor needed to be sped up because I would get too tired. He said he needed to break the amniotic sac with the dreaded hook that looked like a knitting needle. The AmniHook. And then the intravenous drip of Pitocin was started. Doctors call it "the Pit." It's a hormone that speeds up labor contractions and can make them suddenly more excruciating. My pain became unbearable a few minutes later. And now I knew. The pain of birth was like being killed by a piano slowly being lowered on top of you. There was no screaming. You couldn't scream. You were being crushed to death. The epidural man showed up. He told me that my back looked prettier than Susan Sarandon's back. He inserted the tube of anesthesia into my spine, and soon I was completely numb from waist to toes. Another tube was inserted to remove urine from my bladder. An oxygen mask was added to my face, and I was told to lie on my left side to give more oxygen to the baby. I was in the middle of the birth of my nightmares. Hours passed. I lay there listening to loud oxygen-mask Darth Vader breathing sounds. The doctor was in another room. Maybe napping. Maybe chatting. What do they do during cervical dilation?

—The baby's not happy where she is right now. We have to get her out.

I was trying to push but couldn't feel anything because of the epidural anesthesia. They were pushing back my legs in a grotesque tug of war. Forceps clamped onto the baby's head. Loud voices. Bad lighting. Trying to get her out. Dragging her out by her head with metal tongs.

And then it was very quiet.

I was in a place of deep terror, making quiet whining sounds for someone to tell us about the baby. No response.

Many doctors talking very quickly and quietly. More people were in the room now. Emergency doctors had been summoned.

The baby was silent. Was the baby dead? Nobody was talking to us. No time. Just saving the baby. And then she was gone. Out of the room.

Newborn baby with a team of doctors. Bloody room. No baby. Ruin. Birthing music still in the canvas bag with the portable stereo. The happy birthing bag. Rubber rain boots nearby. Silent husband sitting in chair. Alone in this room. No information about the baby. My mother had to be called. She was twelve blocks away waiting to hear the happy news. She didn't even know that the baby had been named after her many months before. Lueza. *Loo-ee-zuh*. A strange spelling passed down from a long-ago ancestor. Lueza Wanda. *Vanda*. She would be named for both grandmothers. One American. One Polish. One living. One dead. Both born in 1931. But I didn't know if she was going to survive her birth and thought maybe we should change the name. Lueza Wanda was not going to die on her birthday. Maybe this baby girl should quickly get another name. Husband made the call. He told my mother that Lueza Wanda had been born but that something had happened and she couldn't breathe and had been taken away to the NICU, where doctors could take care of her. Intensive care for mostly tiny babies who had been born much too early. Babies who could fit in your hand. Our baby was big and healthy looking. She was born exactly nine months to the day after her conception on that frozen afternoon in January.

We were left alone. I remember the anesthesiologist coming back to the silent and bloody room to check on me and Marek; his kindness made me fall toward his chest weeping. I remember someone coming in and giving us a piece of paper with the baby's footprints on them. Perfect tiny black footprints. I had always hated my feet and now I had given birth to a daughter whose feet were perfect.

I was taken to another floor at about one in the morning. I requested that I not be put with the happy new mothers. I wanted to be with women who were suffering. Women who had been cut open. I didn't want to be near nursing mothers. I didn't want to be near women planning circumcisions. They found a room for me away from the joyful mothers. When the epidural wore off at about three and I was able to move, we went to the NICU to find our baby. Lulu was lying naked on her back in a clear plastic crib with a small black piece of excrement between her legs. There must have been many wires attached to her for monitoring vital signs, but I can't remember. I can't remember if she was still attached to the respirator. I remember feeling something between catatonia and terror. I remember asking for an electric breast pump. I remember asking the night nurse to fill me with sleep drugs and to please keep me away from the new mothers with healthy babies.

There Were No Tulips

Lueza started nursing as we weaned her off the barbiturates that stopped her seizures. She woke up. She cried for the first time when the nurse gave her a bath in the sink of the NICU near her plastic crib. When Lueza was twelve days old we were allowed to take her home. The last night at the hospital we slept with Lueza in the Bonding Room. It was a separate room next to the NICU where parents could spend time alone with their baby. Many times it was used for parents of babies who would die or had just died. This was the new way. Babies who died were named and sometimes photos were taken. Parents were encouraged to spend time with the dead baby. I approved of this kind of cathartic experience, but our baby had survived. We were bonding with our living baby and making sure she could nurse. She slept at the foot of our bed in a transparent plastic crib and woke a couple of times in the night and was able to nurse. It was thrilling. We were escaping the nightmare world of sick and dying babies. All we knew was that we would wean her off the barbiturates. No more seizures, no more barbiturates. The doctors told us nothing. We probably had a follow-up appointment with one of their neurologists but were planning on leaving this terror behind because, hey, some births are kind of scary. She would be fine.

We walked out of the hospital with Lu in one of those giant old-fashioned baby carriages. It had been left at my parents' apartment by my older brother, and we had walked it up to the hospital for the great escape. It was a balmy New York October day. Yellow leaves and yellow light and soft humid air. I felt like we had escaped from Hell. We walked down through Central Park to my parents' apartment. I can't remember if we had discussed moving in or if it just happened. Why didn't we walk across the park to our one bedroom on West Eighty-Sixth Street? I do not remember. We had stayed with my parents while Lueza was in the hospital because it was a ten-minute walk away. It seemed natural to go back. We had been married in that living room five years earlier. I had grown up in the middle bedroom, where I had dressed for my wedding. I had hidden my bong in one of the closets. What had happened to that bong? It wasn't easy to throw away a twelve-inch plastic bong. Maybe it was still on the top shelf in that long shipping box. I had hidden my tiny black book of secret thoughts in the air-conditioner. I had accidentally crushed my longest finger in the bathroom door when trying to escape my older brother. This was the bathroom where I cut small slices into my left thumb with a fresh razor blade on the worst days of growing up.

I would see my obstetrician one more time before realizing that I had been sewn up incorrectly after the episiotomy and that maybe Lueza wasn't going to recover from her birth insult. *Insult* was the word that I had heard from our new pediatrician. *Insult* sounded okay. *Insults* aren't permanent.

It was a very clear moment when I knew that things were not going to work out. When Lueza was about one month old I was nursing her in my sister's old bedroom and all of a sudden her head flew back and off my nipple. Her arms went straight up in the air. I didn't want to scare her, but I was terrified and so crushed with dread that I wanted to start shrieking. I knew instinctively that this was some sort of abnormal brain seizure. I knew it was the end of hope.

It didn't look that bad. Lueza's arms would fly up in the air all of a sudden as if she were conducting a particularly dramatic moment in a symphony. Leonard Bernstein mixed with Martha Graham. Sometimes she would smile when it happened. Sometimes she would accidentally scratch her face with tiny fingernails that I was afraid to cut. We went back to the first neurologist and many wires were attached to her head as they observed her brain waves on an endless rolling sheet of paper that a technician monitored. When she started jerking her arms during the EEG, the technician quickly paged the neurologist in the next room and said that he should see what was happening, but he didn't come into the room. He met with us after the test and while staring at my milk-filled breasts told us to take her home and love her. Don't read too much, he said. And he put her back on phenobarbital. This was a huge relief because she started sleeping better at night and wouldn't scream for the three hours before bedtime. I would wander around my parents' apartment doing the bouncy mommy walk and tell her that if she didn't stop crying we would give her to the gypsies. Sometimes my mother would hold her and sing Carmen Miranda songs. Nothing helped.

Lu would cry so much when she was out with our "nanny helper" in the park that people would stare, so I printed up an information card that our "nanny helper" would hand to the rudest of the starers. It stated that the baby was doing the best she could and indeed had suffered neurologically and the family understood how uncomfortable it was to hear a baby crying but that it was good for the child to be outside and to please respect their privacy. I was never in the park when the cards were handed out. I was at home enjoying my time away from the endless screaming. I was writing in my new computer journal of despair.

Three neurologists in a row said the same thing. A rare seizure disorder called infantile spasms. There was one possible cure. It was a hormonal treatment called ACTH and it involved intramuscular injections into her thighs twice a day for one month. It sometimes worked, but they didn't know why. We would have to move into the hospital and learn how to inject the baby and then how to monitor her for all the medical complications that might occur. My husband knew that he could do the injections, which was fortunate because I was too sad to stick a needle into her baby legs. You needed to grab Lu's thigh and squeeze the muscle away from the bone and stick in the needle and pull back the plunger of the syringe to make sure you hadn't hit a vein. Morning and night. The nurses showed Marek how to do injections, and he did them. The nurses were very impressed. I slept next to Lueza in a chair that turned into a bed. Lulu and I shared a room with another mother and her ten-year-old son, who was severely disabled. His body was as thin as a spider and deformed with spasticity. His feet bent back the wrong way, and his head hung over the side of his massive black wheelchair. They were in the hospital to treat his seizures that had become too frequent. I was in awe of the mother. I eavesdropped on an intake one morning with a young doctor and this mother. What I remember most are two things. The doctor asked if the boy had said anything that morning, and the mother responded that he couldn't speak. And I remember the mother saying that he was a "pretty regular kid." I felt that I was in the presence of something holy and that a golden light should fill the room. I pretended that I was reading my magazine. I pretended that this wasn't a foreshadowing event.

We left the hospital after three days, armed with

syringes and a prescription for a tiny bottle of ACTH. We also had to buy a home test kit for feces and urine to make sure that Lueza wasn't going to die from the treatment. I was afraid that she might grow a beard from the hormone. The nurse practitioner had mentioned that the treatment might make her a tad irritable.

It was like dying. After four hours of nonstop crying the first night, my mother found the name of a nursing agency that hired baby nurses for cash-only payment. They came at eight p.m. and left at eight the next morning. They were all Filipina women. One of them had had a child who experienced seizures as a baby and completely recovered. It was going to work out.

During the month of injections, we kept a log of her seizures. I never really understood or wanted to know too much about infantile spasms. What I read at the bookstore was shocking, so I stopped reading. Something about blindness and severe mental retardation. Something about wheelchairs. As the month continued, there were fewer and fewer seizures. And then they stopped.

Lueza's face was huge and swollen with steroids, but she stopped having seizures. She couldn't lift her head up and her hands were always fisted, but she started smiling again. Her new neurologist declared that she had *excellent social skills.* Her eyes followed him during the exam. She smiled at him. She smiled at us. At her next EEG, the doctor informed us that she did not have the dreaded *hypsarrhythmia* pattern of brain waves that often accompanies infantile spasms and usually means a catastrophic prognosis of severe disability.

I was euphoric. From then on, the only question I asked her doctors was: "Can she still be okay?" It was my mantra. Just give me hope and I can live.

A Baby Exercises

Physical therapy for a baby. It sounded reasonable. The state of New York had decided they would send a therapist to visit us at home. Extra help for a baby who had had a difficult birth. She needed exercises to catch up. The seizures might have temporarily scrambled her new brain. I needed to learn new words—*asymmetrical tonic neck reflex, head lag, positioning, muscle tone*. Two familiar words—*muscle tone*—but when put together and spoken by a physical therapist about Lu my chest cavity hurt and I wanted to run.

Lueza was on the high four-poster bed in my old pink bedroom. We were still living with my parents. My stomach was rigid as I watched this kind woman hold Lu's flexed legs and slowly turn her from side to side. What was this woman looking for? Was she going to tell me something bad? The woman seemed delighted with this baby. I didn't ask any questions. If I didn't ask questions, hopefully she wouldn't say anything frightening. We both smiled at the baby. Rocking her side to side. Lueza was calm. I was terrified. My baby was having physical therapy. Something had happened. There were "delays" in her physical baby milestones. Her hands were still tightly fisted most of the time. That was bad for some reason. She couldn't hold her head up at all. In time, I told myself. These things would come in time. That's why this nice woman was moving my daughter on my childhood bed in my parents' apartment. And when the woman used the word *tone*, this time without the word *muscle* in front of it, my gut pulled in and my brain registered the word. Why was a physical therapist mentioning muscle tone? What did muscle tone have to do with a baby? I kept smiling at the woman. A closed-lip smile. Frozen behind my eyes. The word stuck in my amygdala.

The Fifth Neurologist

The neurologist put the MRI of Lueza's brain up on the x-ray light box. I watched his long fingers as he slid each image into the rubber grippers. He had a melanoid Mediterranean bookish kind of handsome with wire-rimmed spectacles. His name was Abba. I liked the name. Abba sounded like the name of a wise man. An ancient man who prayed in the desert. Or was it the name of God? I wanted him to love me and my daughter.

He was our fifth neurologist in six months. When he first ordered the MRI, I didn't want to know anything about the results. He had told me there were some abnormalities, but nothing more was said because the only question I asked him was, "Can she still be alright?" I remember Abba saying, "Yes." She could still be okay. Lueza was about six months old, and I had no idea of where we were neurologically. Would her walking be affected? What about her speech? Would the seizures return?

I had taken the taxi up to the top of Manhattan by myself this time to finally hear what was wrong with my daughter's brain. I wanted to be alone with the neurologist. I wanted him to be clear and blunt, and I didn't want Marek to be there. I wanted to be his translator for this information. Abba pointed out different areas of her brain and showed me where the strokes had occurred. Basal ganglia damaged. I had recently read about basal ganglia at Barnes & Noble. It was very important to have undamaged basal ganglia. Something to do with controlling movement. He pointed out other areas on the MRI film. A splotch here and a white spot there. Milky areas that meant bad things had happened. Tiny newborn strokes. A catastrophic birth.

I nodded my head. I asked a few questions. Abba was good. He didn't tell me anything horrible. No predictions about the future. It was time to go. Time to put the pictures away.

Time to get a cab to go home and tell my husband that it didn't look so good. We had been holding out hope because of this phrase we had recently learned: "the plasticity of the brain." The brain supposedly had an amazing ability to adapt and rewire itself. I had even read an article about a little girl who was having such terrible epileptic seizures that they removed half of her brain and she was just fine. She could walk and talk and play. I was thrilled when I read this story. Having an entire brain was good, but if one could do well without half, then anything was possible.

Now it seemed clear that the plasticity of the brain wasn't really working out. I got into a cab that smelled of rotten candy. We raced down the West Side Highway. I clutched the leathery taxi hand loop and thought about our daughter.

Your child's brain is not supposed to be on a light box. You're not supposed to know anything about it. You're supposed to worry about diaper rash and cradle cap. Bowel movements. Preschools.

I would never sleep again.

I hated the world and everyone in it.

You Will Try

You will try: craniosacral therapy, chiropractic treatments, osteopathy, the laying on of hands, praying, incense, holy powder dust from an Indian guru, hyperbaric oxygen therapy, shrieking, self-injury, threatening suicide, begging, and catatonia.

You will watch your husband lick the head of your seventy-day-old baby, who has started having seizures again, and you will be grateful that this is your husband and he is trying to heal your baby with animal ways. And one day you will find a medical malpractice lawyer with a toasty brown tan and a Brooklyn accent who will read the birth records and the pediatric reports and get you a settlement to pay for the lifetime of caregiving that your child will need.

We Lived Our Life with Nannies

We had money from a settlement.

The hospital and the obstetrician's lawyers offered us money to avoid a trial because of what Lueza's birth record revealed.

The birth record of my contractions and her heartbeats and where it all went bad.

And what about the forceps?

We will never know.

We got the money when Lu was two years old.

Not the kind of money you read about when there is a trial but enough money to get help and then more help.

There were women from the Philippines, Poland, Hungary, France, Slovakia, Colombia, Ecuador, El Salvador, Bosnia, Mexico, England, Guatemala, and the United States.

They were kind and patient and funny and joyful. They had had medical catastrophes and horrific family tragedies and bad husbands and better boyfriends.

I loved these women.

This is how we did it.

Judge Jody

I was a harsh judge. I noticed everything. If I was sitting across from someone on the subway who was barefoot in sandals I would inspect their feet. I would stare at the toes. The toenails were almost trance-inducing. Sometimes the nails curled over the ends of the toes like armor. I would wonder how someone with such sad feet could display them in public. Did they not know how grotesque they were? Why didn't they hide them?

I hated my feet. I pretended they were different by arching and pointing them.

I didn't want to be a cruel judge. I knew how ugly it was to have these thoughts, but it was like a voice inside my head that would just say things when people passed by. Huge fat fanny walking by. Big flat feet with monkey toes. Man with hair plugs. I felt compassionate toward the suffering masses, but I also noticed every blackhead constellation and skin tag on their face.

As I walked down West End Avenue with Lueza in her *therapeutic stroller* with a headrest and an airplane-style seatbelt I was Happy Accepting Mother with Crippled Child. I was not looking out of my eyes at the sidewalk traffic but watching myself as I pushed Lu toward the physical therapist on Riverside Drive. I knew people were staring unless they were too oblivious to notice the beautiful tilting child strapped into her oversized reclining high-tech stroller. I was careful to arrange my facial features into a serene look so that the mothers of hopping, dancing children would not pity me. I brightened my eyes and smiled what I hoped looked like the smile of a wise loving woman who was deeply at peace. If the stranger stared at Lueza, I would watch the staring woman and stop pushing until the woman passed next to us, unaware of the staring mask on her face, then I would bark HELLO and the unaware, staring, pity-filled stranger would come back to reality and wonder why the mother of this crippled child was so belligerent.

Before Lueza, I don't ever remember seeing crippled children in wheelchairs. I probably would have averted my eyes if I had. I would have looked away because who can bear to see a child in a wheelchair? Like passing Zwail's, the fish market on Madison Avenue, when I walked to school. My nose just automatically stopped breathing as I passed.

I'd always been fascinated with fictional crippled children. There was something undeniable about a crippled child. Dickens understood this. Tiny Tim in *A Christmas Carol* and Smike in *Nicholas Nickleby*. We are crippled on the inside, and they are crippled on the outside and sometimes very serene. Unless of course they're suffering from terrible pain, and then serenity is not part of the picture. My favorite play in drama school was *A Day in the Death of Joe Egg* by Peter Nichols about a severely disabled child who is nonverbal and prone to seizures. I was transfixed with the suffering of the mother.

And what about the children? I always wondered: Why can't they walk? What went wrong?

After my daughter was born, when it was completely unclear what would happen, I saw crippled children everywhere. Tiny children in enormous black wheelchairs. Once at the Metropolitan Museum of Art, I saw a woman with two children in wheelchairs. Twins. She and her husband were walking through the museum pushing their two children. They looked European.

I think they were smiling.

I knew that it couldn't happen to me because I would go crazy.

I remember her first wheelchair. First there had been the *therapeutic stroller* when Lueza was about two. A rolling chair that sort of looked like a regular stroller but more technical. More belts and side supports and a shelf to rest her feet. Kind of a wheelchair-in-training. A couple of years later a new therapist was summoned for a *seating evaluation,* and in two months she returned with the newly arrived authentic my-child-will-never-walk-sit-or-hold-up-her-head wheelchair. Seventy pounds of joy. With all the beauty of an electric chair on wheels. Black on black. The Quickie Zippie. When I was alone with this vinyl and metal monstrosity for the first time, I fell forward onto my knees, grabbed the black metal and leatherette armrests, and wept. It's a big step to get the first wheelchair.

It's one of the milestones.

A real fire walk.

Why I Want to Be a Buddhist

I was reading a book about anger. It was written by a famous Buddhist monk. The main thing was breathing mindfully through your anger. No hitting of pillows. No screaming. Just breathing. It was such a different approach from my father's philosophy. He had explained to us when we were children that unless he expressed his anger he would have terrible back pain. You had to let it out or you would get migraines and crippling lumbar spasms. So objects were thrown and doors were lashed with umbrellas. Headboards were throttled. Mugs and mustardy hot dogs were flung. Despite this method, every couple of months, our father would get a migraine and disappear into my parents' darkened bedroom and remain motionless on the bed with pillows over his head. We would tiptoe around until he emerged. He would look stunned, and we would feel sad. He would walk to the piano and play Chopin nocturnes.

Our mother, who never seemed to get angry, would make a tinfoil-wrapped onion soup pot roast from the *I Hate to Cook Cookbook*. Father would watch old WWII movies from the vibrating fake leather recliner with our beloved clawless neutered Siamese cat Ping on his lap.

I was troubled by my own anger. I was troubled by my personality. It seemed unpleasant and lacking in grace. I felt that I carried a bad seed. I yelled at my husband when he lost things. I yelled at him when I found the secret pile of three years of unread *New Yorkers*. When we got lost in the rental car in London in 1988 and I thought we would be killed, I screamed. When Lueza's wheelchair broke, I clutched my head and dug my fingernails deep into my scalp. I was a shrew.

The Buddhist monk had called anger "a seed" in his book. I liked the metaphor. Apparently, I had been watering the seed too much. I had been cultivating it. Growing it. I needed to breathe more. I needed to greet it like a sad familiar friend who was stopping by for a short visit.

I decided to meditate. I closed my eyes and started to count breaths. The inhalations were on the odd numbers and the exhalations were even. I went up to ten and then back to one. My heart was thumping in my chest cavity. I decided to visualize a mountain. A green mountain. Majestic. Without cliffs. I hoped it would calm my breathing. I added some water to the image. If only I had been raised in India. I wanted a religion crammed full of ritual. I loved the word *temple*. Filled with incense and Indian raga music. Pujas in the home. Incense burning in every corner. Pasty substances to smear on your forehead. Ritual bowls of food. The corner where ancestors were honored with offerings of food and prayers. Amulets and beads and candles. Every life transition with its own very specific prayers. Chanting and meditation. May I be well. May I be peaceful. I usually inserted: *May I be free from self-loathing. May I have self-compassion. May I realize that I'm going to die and Get Over Myself.*

My heart started doing that fluttery thing. A bird stuck in my chest. Butterflies in the heart. Why hadn't I become an expert in something? Why wasn't I a doctor? A nephrologist. A pediatric neurologist. A person who saved lives. Why couldn't I concentrate? My thoughts were a swarm of flies. I stopped counting my breaths and focused on the word *peace*.

I felt that I was suffocating. I opened my eyes and focused on a spot on the rug in front of me. It was a kind of Zen meditation I had read about. You are supposed to keep your eyes open. I thought it might help me feel less panicky. A spider raced across the floor in front of me. I flattened it with my boiled wool slipper. I worried about Lueza. I worried about cancer. Maybe something was growing undetected in my body. I did have that new pain in my back that had never been there before. It was different from the icepick in the back right ribs that I frequently felt. It might be a spinal cancer. Or metastases from another tumor. Maybe that was why I was so interested in death. It was a premonition. I had flown on Pan Am Flight 103 three weeks before it blew up over Scotland. A high school classmate had been on the doomed flight. Now it was my turn. I was going to die soon. I would set the example for a Natural Death in my community. I would order a cardboard coffin through the internet. I would decorate it. Wasting away surrounded by family and friends. I would be the best dying person.

—Peachie . . .

Marek called me Peachie. I called him Peachie.

—Peachie. You are an artist. You need another job in the theater.

Another kind of husband would have condemned me and told me that I was mentally ill. He would've divorced me.

—Thank you, Peachie.

He stroked my head with his large soft hand. Starting at my forehead and back to the occipital joint. Over and over.

Sanatorium

I think there should be a place to go when you feel like injuring yourself. When you have an overwhelming need to start ripping your garments and clawing at your face but you know you won't do it. There should be a place.

Not an ugly lockdown psychiatric ward kind of place but a place like something in a European movie. Kind people taking care of you. Reclining on wooden deck chairs swaddled in blankets gazing at mountains while gentle nurses bring cups of tea. You would go to treatment rooms and receive massages and soak in hot tubs with therapeutic waters. Blind Mongolian healers would press their fingers into your spine. There would be no loud talkers. You could walk around in soft cloth robes and slippers made of special fibers. At night, you would sit by the fire and learn about constellations and dark matter.

Each day you would feel stronger, and one day it would be decided by the wise old doctor that you were ready for the mountain walks where wildflowers were gathered.

In the evening, you would sit by the fire. An

elderly crone would bring you a small book filled with illustrations and descriptions of the local mountain flora. You would hold it in your hands and realize that you really did want to live in this world. You would be healed by nature and kind people with European accents and soft hands.

The Yes People

I knew there were happy women out there. Women who were making homemade pickles and chutneys. Women who knew what a winter garden was. Women who could make their child's Halloween costume and throw a birthday party for twelve little girls without feeling nauseated. Women for whom a piñata represented a fun thing at a birthday instead of a threat that a child would be brain damaged by a swinging bat. There were women out there who were doctors and mothers at the same time. Women who were running companies and going to green markets on Sundays and writing books of short stories while their children napped.

When I made soup, I felt like one of the happy people. A sensation would shoot straight through me for a couple of seconds, and I would almost feel blissful as I poured a handful of brown rice into the steaming pot of turkey soup that my husband had made after Thanksgiving. I hadn't made the soup, but I had thrown in the handful of rice, and I had watched and tended it, and it almost felt like it was my soup. I felt ecstatic when I chopped onions and scraped them off the special wooden cutting board that was used only for onions and garlic and watched them fall into the frying pan with olive oil and make the sound of rain as they hissed and smelled and transformed the kitchen into a place where people cooked meals and drank red wine and life was lived.

A Bad Wife

—Marek. You just ate it. It's in your stomach. Your large intestine is full of food from a day ago.

—Peachie, you don't know what you're talking about. That salad is giving me sraczka.

Roll the tongue on the 'R' so it's *sa-rachka*. Polish for diarrhea.

—But the salad is in your stomach! Do you know anything about DIGESTION?

We frequently had this argument. How long did it take? How was it related to gas in the intestine? How long did it take for food to become gas? For solid matter to turn into noxious air? I would check my medical books. I have a collection of heavy health reference books to check on all of my various symptoms. I know I have tendencies toward hypochondria, but I'm not a hypochondriac, because I am aware of these leanings. I loved reading about medicine. Whenever someone I know gets cancer I read up on the symptoms and treatments. When my gallbladder was removed, I asked the doctor to save my gallstones. I have always regretted not asking the gynecologic surgeon to save the honeydew melon–sized cyst from my left ovary. I was thirteen and hadn't thought to ask him. I imagined it floating in a glass jar high on a shelf in the basement of New York Hospital. My grotesque and precious cyst. A dermoid cyst. A benign ovarian tumor. A teratoma. The Latin word for monster. The cells can form themselves into any dermal tissue. Many contained long hairs and sebaceous material. Some have fully formed teeth or an eyeball. Forty years later, I searched Google for images and scrolled through the glistening medical photos. My little monster. I was told that I was supposed to be a twin and instead I got a cyst.

—Marek. What do you know about food in the gut? It takes HOURS and HOURS for food to become WASTE!

—Stop it, Peachie. You don't know what you're talking about. Unless it's in the *New York Times* you don't think it exists.

I was never meant to be a wife.

Extreme Breastfeeding

When Lueza was two years and ten days old her sister Dora was born. We had chosen a different doctor and a different hospital. We found a birthing teacher. What I really wanted for this birth was to go to The Farm in Tennessee with all the hippie midwives and have the most famous hippie midwife deliver this child, but I knew I would give birth in a hospital.

It was a warm Saturday in October, and I was facing out the back of the taxi supported by pillows and yelling as the contractions opened my cervix and pushed the baby down. I remember seeing Macy's as we headed south. I was yelling: the baby's coming out, the baby's coming out. Full dilation in a New York City taxi. Marek and Risa, the birthing teacher, saying something encouraging to try and make me believe that I could do this. When we arrived on the labor and delivery floor, the youngish obstetrician on call was leaning his buttocks against a desk, arms folded on a soft belly. It was Saturday and unfortunately he had to work.

—Where have you been? I've been waiting here for an hour.

I had miscalculated the amount of time it would take to get to the hospital. It had taken much longer to get out of our apartment in the storm of high labor. The pain was like death. For some reason I insisted on finding a particular brown hair scrunchy to keep my hair off my face. I worried about which shoes to put on with the baggy green leggings that my friend Elizabeth had given me in the last weeks of this pregnancy. And then we had to find a taxi on West End Avenue and drive seventy blocks southeast in Manhattan.

We got into the birthing room and the doctor suggested I take a shower to relax. Risa urged him to check me. He discovered that the baby was about to come out and there would be no bathing.

I had always wanted to squat for birth, but I was lying on my right side and the birth was happening. Marek was standing next to the doctor and peering at Dora's head as it emerged. He took one of those squashed baby-head photos that modern fathers take and nobody wants to see. Three pushes and she was out. Her cord had ripped off but she was strong and healthy and howling. The doctor with attitude said something about needing to warm her, and I watched him rub her vigorously under heating lamps before handing her over and beginning the patchwork stitching on my torn perineum. The baby lay on my chest, and I could see the doctor between my legs like a tailor with thread. I wanted the phone. Everyone had been terrified about this baby's birth. My husband

and I had never been frightened. We figured that the odds were in our favor and that there was no reason a second baby would be brain damaged at birth. My uterus was not a death zone.

I never imagined that I was the kind of woman to be an extreme breastfeeder. I knew that I wanted to nurse my babies, but one year seemed sufficient. Before I had children, I babysat for my best friend's two-year-old and was shocked when he woke from his nap and started grabbing at my breast saying: nurse just a little, nurse just a little! Maybe this was too much love.

Once I started, I could not stop. I loved the animal kingdom pleasure of it. You could feed your baby like a beast. I learned how to nurse and sleep. I didn't care what the experts said. I knew that a baby didn't need a room of her own. Babies didn't need to learn how to sleep alone. I cared deeply about my own exhaustion and the quickest way to get back to sleep after Dora woke at two in the morning was to lie on my left side and let her nurse until we were asleep. Breastfeeding was easier than formula. You didn't have to sterilize or measure or warm. I was a human pacifier and loved it. Instant joy and comfort. Even when there was no milk left, Dora would suck before going to bed at night or when she screamed from a needle stick at the pediatrician.

And then one day Mommy had to go to the emergency room for excruciating pain in her chest and upper back. I didn't come home for an entire week. I returned without a gall bladder and with a puffy air-filled post-laparoscopy belly full of strong drugs and explained to my three-and-a-half-year-old daughter that there could be no more nursing. And so it ended.

Sex had ended for me, too. I had no interest in it. I couldn't stand being touched. I wanted the closeness with the babies, but I didn't want the other kind of closeness that had produced the babies. I can't remember when it stopped. I only remembered that the bed had become a sacred place for sleep. I remember being told by a therapist that I saw once or twice that I should get the baby out of our bed. That this was important for the marriage. Remove baby from bed.

I chose Dora. Maybe it was because something catastrophic had happened to Lueza that I wanted to keep Dora close. Maybe I wanted to slow time down and not miss anything with this baby who I was able to take care of without a team of doctors and therapists. Maybe I wanted to get some sleep. Maybe I just didn't care. It was over for me. I didn't want a new husband, I just wanted to be left alone. When I heard the older couple in the apartment above us having sex, it seemed ridiculous. I tried to imagine myself having a love affair and thrashing around in sweatiness and desire, but I could not be that woman. I was Mommy.

School

Lueza started school when she was three. There must have been meetings with the New York Board of Education, where it was decided that she would start at United Cerebral Palsy.

What is cerebral palsy?

It has something to do with brain damage. Usually. Brain damage to parts of the brain that control movement and muscle tone.

Did Marek drive us down to East Twenty-Third Street from Ninetieth Street and West End Avenue?

Did we take a taxi?

How did we collapse the therapeutic stroller into the cab while leaving Lueza on a taxi seat?

I do not remember.

And what did Lueza think?

I remember the big awning that said United Cerebral Palsy. I remember calming Lu down with singing and getting her settled into a therapy chair in the classroom. Therapy chair meant straps and pads and belts to support her in a sitting position so she wouldn't need to be held like a baby. She could sit up in a circle of children. She could be a student.

And I could sneak out, cross Twenty-Third Street and head to Einstein Bros. Bagels for a large coffee with cream and a toasted, buttered poppy seed bagel as I waited to pick her up a few hours later.

Or maybe Marek picked her up with the Subaru.

I do not remember.

I do remember finding a section of the *New York Times* one day on a table where I ate my bagel and reading it because it was the weekday arts section about a rock concert benefit for a special school for children with severe speech and physical disabilities, and it had something to do with Neil Young and his son. When Lu was a baby, my friend Elizabeth kept telling me that Neil Young also had a child with cerebral palsy, and I had always wanted to know what the story was. How were they doing? How did families do this?

The review described an outdoor rock concert somewhere in California. They described the children on stage in wheelchairs behind the band. The children were facing the audience. The children were happy. They described little communication devices attached to their wheelchairs. Computers that could *speak for* children without speech. The musicians could turn upstage and play to the children and give them their drumsticks and high-five them at the end of their sets. They described children like Lueza.

Three years later we moved to California.

Moving the Gallstones

After I had my gallbladder removed in 2000, I held the tiny gallstones between my fingers and crushed them to see how hard they were. With enough pressure, they squashed into a sandy dark greenish powder. I put them in a small plastic container and kept them on a shelf in my bedroom in New York. I lost track of them when we moved to California later that year. They are probably in a box in the garage. Many things are still in boxes. The way we left New York was by calling a moving company and paying for the service where everything is done by the movers. They arrived at our apartment on West End Avenue in the early morning with hundreds of flattened boxes and proceeded to put every single object into a box until the apartment had disappeared. I kept a small suitcase with my necklaces and bracelets and important documents but everything else was gone. The next morning the driver from the moving company arrived and loaded the truck. I had never imagined leaving New York City. It had always been unthinkable, but in the past two years I knew it was time to go, and when Lueza got into Bridge School we made our move.

We arrived in San Mateo, California, on August 15, 2000. San Francisco was seventeen miles north. I put the pots and pans and dishes and utensils in the kitchen, my clothes in our bedroom, the children's things in their drawers, and I never wanted to go back into the garage for the other twenty-seven boxes. There are boxes filled with old stuffed animals that never made it upstairs and toys that should have been thrown away. My collection of plays and theater books from college. Old sheet music for auditions. Black and white resumé photos from about five different photographers. I kept them hidden in the old box that had now crossed the country. A box of love letters from an older French man who is probably dead. He fed me stinky cheese and French baguette on a nude beach near Italy. Letters from a short love affair with a man who had died from electrocution on the wet stone floor of a chateau in Normandy. Love letters from my Polish husband. All of my old journals are down there. Embarrassing collections of alienation and whiny depression. The despair of the privileged. I cannot read them, but I cannot discard them. Maybe I will request that they be burned at my death. I don't want my daughter to know who I was.

Why I'm Attracted to Mortuary Work

I had been planning Lueza's funeral ever since her classmate Leah died in 2002. I was searching on the internet. Leapfrogging from one death website to another. The burning ghats of India. The Jewish burial rituals of Tahara. The green funeral movement. Willow coffins. Burial shrouds without coffins. Forest burials without gravestones. You could find the spot with satellite technology. I also did research about the process of embalming and how the funeral industry convinced people it was necessary. It wasn't. And the marketing of coffins. And grave liners that you would put in the ground and place the coffin inside of with the guarantee of absolutely no leakage. The body would remain intact forever. I ended up at a website for a mortuary school. It used to be in San Francisco but they had to move farther east because of San Francisco's real estate boom. So many interesting classes. Anatomy. The cultural study of death. Bereavement. Death doulas. Maybe I would start a nonprofit anti-funeral-business organization. Help people take death back into the home.

Lueza was almost eight. Leah had just turned eleven years old. She had also been brain damaged at birth. Like Lueza, she couldn't hold her body upright or speak. They had similar wheelchairs. Seatbelts and padded side supports held them in a sitting position. They both required neck supports and headrests to be upright. They were both beautiful. Leah had been in school on Monday, and on Friday night she died at a San Francisco hospital. When I drove into the school parking lot on Friday afternoon to pick up Lueza, one of the classroom assistants was standing outside waiting. Something was wrong. The assistant came up to the wheelchair van window and told me that Leah had suddenly become ill with a vicious pneumonia in the last two days and was probably going to die later that night and the mother wanted to make sure that I knew because we were friends and Lu adored the mom and we had eaten strata at their home and I was good friends with the cousin of the little girl and had actually heard about this child many years before we knew we would move to California and end up at the same school. I saw another mother next to my car who had also heard the news. We stood in the parking lot and grabbed each other's hands. I brought Lueza home to Marek and headed into San Francisco to be with Leah and her family for a brief hour of the hospital vigil.

The next time this happened I received a message on the answering machine from another parent about a child who had just graduated from Lu's school that spring. I phoned back and was told that she had died in the middle of the night unexpectedly during an illness. I remember screaming. It was a combination of screaming, crying, and falling to the linoleum floor. The girl had just started at our local high school. She looked very much like Lueza. I had been very hopeful for Lu's prospects because of this child. She was five years older. This child was doing great. There was a future for these severely crippled kids.

What was now clear to me was very different, and perhaps everybody knew this.

Our children would not survive.

Picking Daisy

I dreamed that my breasts were leaking milk the night before we picked up the puppy. I was sleeping with Dora in a shiny new Holiday Inn Express a few hours northeast of Los Angeles. Men in cowboy hats with big dry hands rode the elevators. I had driven down with Dora the night before with a tiny green nylon leash and collar and diaper pads to protect the car seat from puppy urine. We had stopped at the big box pet store in the mall before heading east and joining Interstate 5 to take us southeast to the breeder's home on the edge of the desert. Lueza and Dora had been growing up with the weekend dogs of Marek's girlfriend. Dora had grieved the deaths of both dogs by the time she was eight. Lu seemed uninterested in canines. Her hands couldn't pat them or hold them. She couldn't summon them with cooing. I was grateful that Dora was a dog-loving child who could lie on floors with them and lay her head on their dog shoulders. Dogs would bring more love into the house. Dora would be able to physically play with a dog in a way that was impossible for Lu. There could be chasing games. Jumping games. A third child for our family.

This was my first dog. Our childhood pet was a gentle and fat Siamese cat named Ping. Our mother had never wanted a dog. She was taking care of too many humans to want or need another creature other than the self-cleaning cat that arrived mysteriously one night with our father. I had never really cared about dogs. They scared me. Our cousins' dog was a small terrier who was always chasing us if we ran; we made fun of him when our cousins weren't there. We knew that Ping was superior. Ping could jump higher. He had self-possession. There was also the problem of male dogs doing humpy things on little girls that embarrassed and disgusted me. You couldn't trust them. And that horrible red shiny dog penis that would inevitably emerge.

The dog breeder's town was in flash-flood territory. The week before, a child and her mother had been swept away to their deaths. The days before our departure had been rainy and I was wondering if we would survive.

Except for the endless feedlot in Coalinga, which is a place of mass cow suffering and which you can smell for miles before you actually see it in all of its horror, I love Interstate 5. It is the major north–south route of California, and if you want to get to Los Angeles from San Francisco without flying, this is it. Two lanes surrounded by the vastness of California. Once in a while there is a sign for a prison. The land stretches out on either side until it turns into hills to the west and mountains to the east. There are farms and gas stations. It is mostly sky. Now, at the end of February after a big storm, the sky was biblical. Massive cumulus clouds and jutting shafts of angled sunlight. I was not looking forward to the dark. At a certain point, I had to exit the 5 and head east to Palmdale. Straight through the desert and flash-flood world. Dora slept through this final part of our journey to the puppy. I was glad that she slept as I clung to the steering wheel with numb fingers. I could see sections of the road ahead, and by a certain shiny blackness I knew that it was covered in water. I drove slowly into them and through them and wondered what a woman from New York City was doing in a black partially flooded desert at ten o'clock at night.

The breeder's house was on the edge of this isolated desert town. The paved roads became dirt lanes, and houses had high metal fences surrounding them. I could see chickens running and a couple of goats in front of a row of houses. The breeder's house looked brand new. A huge fenced area behind the house contained the kennels. Everything dusty. Mountains to the east. The breeder's husband wore a t-shirt and sweatpants and sat barefoot in a faux leather reclining chair watching a football game. The breeder told us to choose our dog from the four female puppies that were clustered in the playpen. They were a mix of golden retriever and white poodle. Planned mutts. The early days of the goldendoodle craze. The look was a cross between a sheep dog and a terrier. It was like falling in love. I reached into the pen and picked up the largest puppy and inhaled her neck. Not wanting the biggest dog of the litter, I lifted a smaller pup and passed her to Dora and asked if this was our Daisy. And it was done. Papers were signed and wads of cash were presented. Before we drove away, I took the towel to the metal fence where Daisy's mother clamored to make contact. The breeder had suggested bringing a towel that could be rubbed with the mother dog's scent to comfort the trauma of the puppy leaving home. Fool the puppy with smells of mother. But she wasn't an orphan. She was ours. We would love her forever.

Bedtime

I sat on the couch picking the dog's toenails. Peeling little layers of dog nail from the side of the claw and flicking them onto the rug. It relaxed me. It distracted me from the screaming. Bedtimes were not going well anymore. They could now take three hours.

Three hours of going in and out of the room. Lueza would be quiet for fifteen minutes, and then the yelling would start. Sometimes the yelling turned into shrieking. The shrieking produced a writhing movement, and she would rotate counterclockwise on her futon. After a ten-minute session of this attempted communication and movement, Lu would be covered in sweat and I would have to take everything off and change her into fresh pajamas. Sometimes the yelling happened because there was a diaper that needed to be changed.

Sometimes it was a specific CD that Lu wanted. She went through phases. There was the *Sound of Music* phase. She watched the DVD obsessively, including all the supplemental material. Interviews with Julie Andrews and Christopher Plummer in front of a fireplace. I thought of them now as Julie and Chris.

They were family. The actors who played the von Trapp Family children and who were now forty years older and sitting on couches talking about their time in Austria. Lulu loved all of it. Then there was the Broadway Kids period. A series of albums featuring a group of kids who were currently starring in Broadway shows. Pint-sized belters and prepubescent crooners. I had worked with one of the kids a long time ago in *The Who's Tommy*. What had ever happened to him, I wondered? A lot of those kids never work again. They grow up and do something sensible. Another favorite musical was *Carousel*. Lueza loved Rodgers and Hammerstein. Her favorite song was "When You Walk through a Storm." It is sung after Billy Bigelow dies. "When you walk through a storm / Hold your head up high / And don't be afraid of the dark." "Walk on, walk on" was the main refrain. I thought that it might be a good song at Lueza's funeral.

I hoped that maybe if I worried enough nothing bad would happen, at least not for a long time. During one of my Google orgies I discovered the website of a statistician whose expertise was predicting the life expectancies of brain-damaged children. He was sometimes used as an expert witness in court cases when they were trying to figure out settlements for kids who had been the victims of medical malpractice. The money people wanted to know how long the child might live and how much money would be needed to take care of them. The results of a huge study done in California on kids with severe physical disabilities didn't look promising for us. Her life expectancy was greatly reduced because of many different factors. She couldn't hold up her head, she couldn't use her hands, she couldn't roll over, and she couldn't sit. Obviously she couldn't sit if she couldn't hold up her head, but I liked the litany of the negative sometimes. I liked the contrast of the bad news to the good news of Lu's spirit. Her extreme joy. Her dark sense of humor. She was *normal* to us.

When I went back to the screaming room I would always ask her what was wrong. Did she have a question? Lueza couldn't speak, but she understood the letters of the alphabet. She was able to indicate *yes* by a turn of the head and *no* with a slight shake back and forth.

I named each letter of the alphabet. On a certain letter she would turn her head quickly to the right and smile or laugh. This meant that this was the first letter of the word that she wanted us to figure out so we could talk to her about some very specific thing. She wanted us to guess what she wanted us to tell her. Did she want to *make* a phone call? An imaginary phone call with an invisible phone had become extremely popular with her. Sometimes Lu wanted to call Elmo. Sometimes it was a real person. The current favorite was the Brazilian boyfriend of our beloved caregiver. I would speak in a fake Brazilian accent, and we would "call" Alex in his cab. For a long time we used to pretend to call a little girl we had met at Disneyland. In real life it was a brief meeting. A short tram ride back to the parking lot with a family that had a daughter who also couldn't speak and was in a wheelchair. Both little girls were strapped in their wheelchairs side by side in the back of the tram. Lulu was craning her head to the right so she could see the girl. Craning and grinning. Her name was Rachel. It was a five-minute tram ride at ten o'clock at night with a family who had a daughter in a wheelchair as well as two able-bodied brothers. I always wondered about them. The little girl's disability was completely different from Lu's, but they were both without speech and traveling in wheelchairs. She would forever be called Disneyland Rachel. For months we would "phone" her before Lulu went to sleep. It was always a little too late to call, but her mom would always "answer" the phone as she was putting Rachel to bed or taking her out of a bath and they would "talk." I would try to get Lulu to do her *yes* sound, and then Disneyland Rachel's mom would praise Lulu for her great abilities of speech.

Sometimes it wasn't a phone call that was desired but a question to be answered.

When the little girls from her school started dying, she became obsessed with *what happened*. She wanted to know. Sometimes it was: how did it happen? She didn't seem upset when I talked about it. She wanted to hear me tell her WHAT HAPPENED over and over. The same details. That the little girl had gotten sick with something REALLY BAD and then it was TOO LATE. They couldn't save her. And that Lu didn't have to worry about it because it was something VERY RARE. I didn't mind talking to her about the deaths because Lu never seemed upset. She needed to hear about it over and over. I would ask Lulu: what was the question? I would say all the words that began with a *w*—was it a *why*, *when*, *what*, or *will* question?—and then wait for Lu to make her *yes* sound. And I would tell the story AGAIN.

The dog was passively letting me peel most of her nails. It was now clear that the screaming would only get worse. It was a clonazepam night. We had a small stash of this benzodiazepine that the pediatrician had prescribed for nights like this. We hardly ever used it, but if the screaming went on for too long and we had already been in and out of her room forever and there wasn't a poop and imaginary phone calls had been made and deaths discussed, then sometimes we gave drugs. I crushed the pill (Why were there no suppositories for people who could barely swallow? Perhaps a nasal spray?) under a spoon on a piece of foil and carefully folded the foil so that it formed a neat little chute to pour the powder straight into a tiny saucer, where it would be mixed with applesauce. It would have to fit into one spoonful because getting her to swallow it was almost impossible. She knew something nasty was coming. I'd sit on the futon with her on my lap, head twisting away and body rigid, and force it into her mouth with the maroon plastic therapy spoon. It was a 2mg dose of clonazepam. Sometimes it seemed to have no effect on her, but eventually she would fall asleep and we were free. She almost never woke up before morning.

I checked the relic under the futon. It was a palm-sized metal picture frame with a tiny scrap of black cloth in the center. Fabric from the garment of a saint. A gift from my mother's best friend. It had been given to us for Lu's protection when she was a baby and it wasn't clear how things would turn out. Just a scary birth story. Everyone had them. "Oh, my child was born with the cord around his neck. It was terrifying!" And all their kids were fine. I loved these stories. So much hope. When it was clear that things were not going to be fine I began hating these tales of faux woe. I wanted to scream at these women. But before the screaming there had still been hope. We had taken Lu for the laying on of hands at St. John the Divine near Columbia University. We had had her blessed by the hugging saint, Amma, at a Universalist Church on the Upper West Side.

I love the hope of miracles. Maybe there had been miracles that we didn't know about. Maybe her survival had been a miracle. Or the fact that she could see. Some babies with brain damage lose their vision. It's called cortical blindness.

Lu had the miracle of a joyful spirit. Despite her tiny frame and the increasing deformity of her spine, she was healthy. She ate by mouth. Everything blended smooth with a miniature food processor. Massive amounts of food. Bowls of roasted sweet potatoes with Irish butter that reminded Marek of the butter from Poland. Huge bowls of spaghetti bolognese and macaroni and cheese. Fresh blended California O'Henry peaches in summer. Sardines with cottage cheese was a favorite. Marek had discovered this option. He is a fish lover. Fresh fish, bottled fish, or fish from tins. He loves it all. I gagged from the sardine smell but knew it was brain and bone food for Lueza, and how had I found such a kind man to marry?

Family Christmas

I helped my husband choose a Christmas present for his girlfriend. It was a pin. Maybe it was a brooch. It was a dark green jewel-like thing that you would fasten to the top of a sweater or a blouse. I would never wear a pin, but I knew that the girlfriend would like it. The girlfriend wore dresses sometimes. She wore stylish little boots. Her blond hair looked completely natural. Later, when she took off the little black boots, I noticed that her feet were well arched and her toenails painted a dark color. I felt like a frumpy American tomboy around her. With sad feet. A few stray hairs on my big toes. Barely arched feet. Feet passed down from the Austro–Hungarian Jews. They are a version of my father's feet, and his are the small feet of his father, whose parents came to New York from Budapest in the late 1800s. My great-grandmother knew how to bake the luscious Hungarian cakes that were eaten in cafés in Budapest. People who knew how to work. People who knew when it was time to leave Europe for America. They knew that going into the arts was ridiculous. Their son, my grandfather, was forbidden from being an actor. He would go into business. He would start a business during the Depression. He would live in hotels with dachshunds. His feet were never a hindrance.

The first time we went to Sylwia's as a family was on a Christmas Day. Sylwia was wearing a long black velvet dress. Old-fashioned looking. She was beautiful. The beauty of a Slavic woman. Her makeup was subtle and moist. We had met several times, but I had never gone to her home for a social visit.

I felt that I was tipping over when we first arrived. My heart was accelerating. Luckily, there were children to look at and presents to put under the tree. The dogs were barking. Lueza's wheelchair poncho needed to be removed. Dora was running to Sylwia for a huge hug and a quick demonstration of new dance steps. I took some quick sneaky glances around the apartment and noticed photographs of my husband with Sylwia from their translation trips. Nothing was hidden from me. Sylwia was kissing Lu and offering tea. I was scooping Lueza out of her wheelchair and supporting her body and head on my lap with my left arm and doing a quick diaper wetness check.

There would be tea. A Christmas lunch would be cooked and eaten. A chicken would be accidentally roasted upside down. Steamed vegetables. Presents would be exchanged. I would secretly open every drawer in the bathroom while I kept the water running. Looking for something private. Drugs or birth control. Creams for yeast infections. Surely Sylwia hadn't reached menopause yet.

Sylwia was two years older than me. I liked Sylwia. It was possible that I liked Sylwia more than I liked my husband. Why did my husband have a wife and a girlfriend sitting at the same table on Christmas Day? This wasn't a French movie, after all, it was real life. I told myself that it was different because I wasn't intimate with my husband anymore. I wasn't the divorce type. It wouldn't be fair to the children. When a friend had suggested that I had an open marriage, I said *no*. It wasn't that. Open marriage seemed to be a step away from swapping and swinging and blow-jobs in public places. I considered myself a devout monogamist. My *situation* had developed over many years. Many years with deep incompatibility. I had my children and theater work and close friends and family, and I couldn't blame Marek. I was a bad wife. My temper was volatile. I was mildly depressed. I was fearful. I knew this. I had no interest in the marriage. The children were everything. We revolved around them like a tiny solar system. Having Christmas Day with the Polish girlfriend made sense. She couldn't be without Marek and the children on this joyous day of presents and carols and the enormous Christmas tree. And I was in love with the man I'd met in the school parking lot, and I would die happy. The suffering had ended, and I was sitting at a Christmas dinner table with two Polish people and a huge glass of wine, feeling the peace of friendship.

We talked about yoga. We talked about backs. I pretended we were all just good friends. Yo-Yo Ma's cello was in the living room speakers. The Christmas tree almost reached the ceiling. A log was burning in the fireplace. A photograph of Warsaw before the war hung near her dining table. There was no clutter. The bookshelves were filled with novels and poetry books. Many English–Polish dictionaries. Photographs of laughing women. Photographs of the girlfriend's two dogs. The home of a single woman without children. The home of a woman who loved my children.

Big Boyfriend

I fell in love with him in the parking lot. The school for children with extreme special needs. The first time I saw this man he was carrying a small boy under his arm like kindling. The man, who had no familial resemblance to the boy, and who appeared too old to be his father, was big. On top of his mountain-man ribcage was an enormous box-like head covered in snowy white hair. His hands were tanned with strong rectangular nail beds. I watched him as he strode up the path, squealing boy under arm, huge flat feet in hiking sandals and gray socks. Some kind of a California man.

Children were being unloaded in wheelchairs from a tiny school bus by an elevator lift or carried out of the backs of cars like giant babies and strapped into wheelchairs. Lueza rode in the center of the miraculous invention called the wheelchair van. Vans adapted specifically for transporting wheelchairs with the rider in a wheelchair bolted to the floor. We had bought the van eight days after arriving in Northern California. The side door would open with the touch of a button, and a folded metal drawbridge would lower to the ground for the wheelchair to exit. It was grand. Our life was transformed. No more back-ripping lifting of wheelchairs. No more weeping and cursing as I tried to fold the therapeutic stroller into the back of a New York City taxi with Lulu lying on a filthy taxi seat.

The boy under the man's arm was making high-pitched shrieking sounds. The joyful screeching of a nonverbal child. He was grinning. There was a brown cowboy kerchief around his neck to wipe his drool-slick chin. I was inspecting the man. After he left the boy lying on his side on a beanbag couch in the classroom, he returned with a small homemade wooden chair and handed it to the teachers. I watched him like a spy and watched myself watching him and wondered why I was so interested in this rugged-looking big-headed man. We both had crippled children. It was intoxicating if you were attracted to nurturing men.

A few days later it was clear that the beautiful shrieking boy also had a mother. Much younger than the lion-haired man. She brought the boy to school later in the week. Always the same days. She referred to the big handsome man as her son's dad. Sam's *dad* was doing such and such with him. She never called him by name. I was hoping they were divorced. He looked too tall for this small woman. They never sat together at school meetings. She looked beautiful and tired. Her laminated identity work badge was always clipped to her shirt, suggesting a routine of racing down freeways between this school and her job and the therapy appointments that punctuated all our lives. She had tiny feet and enormous lips. The lips worried me. In books these lips were always called sensual. If one had sensual lips, was that a guarantee that the possessor of said lips was also sensual. Could you be frigid with voluptuous lips?

I prayed that they were divorced.

A few weeks later, the beautiful boy's father and I talked about orthopedic surgeons and physical therapists.

—Sam has an amazing physical therapist in San Francisco. Would you like to go with us someday?

—Wow. Yes.

—Okay. I'll tell her about Lueza.

The big man had an old name. Henry. He could've been a Noah. Or a Moses. I could picture him in long rough robes striding through the desert on huge leather sandals. A considerable amount of well-shaped bone formed his nose. People would follow this man. Women must love him. I started wondering how he could have become divorced from the beautiful, much younger, overworked pillow-lipped woman. When you had a crippled child to take care of, how could you split open a family? Surely he was a philanderer. He had taught English, and what could be better for a handsome man than an endless supply of adoring young students?

I was glad I figured this out before it was too late. The next clear sign that this man should be avoided was that Sam was leaving the special school to join his local public school at the end of the year. He was graduating and ready for the idealistic plan of "full inclusion." There would be no more parking lot conversations for us to share stories about doctors and surgeries and toilets. Henry was fond of a special-needs toilet seat shaped like a dinosaur that he thought Lueza might be able to use, but I had no faith that toilets would be in Lueza's future, and his enthusiasm squashed me.

He was all tan forearms and strong hands and father energy, and my hypothalamus would send out adrenaline, and my heart would pound when I saw his teal minivan in the school parking lot.

He probably didn't even know my last name. He most likely had a former writing student California goddess with highly arched feet and wet lips kept in a cabin somewhere making him soups and giving him succor. What wife could tolerate a man like this? Thank God he was leaving the special school and I would never see him again.

The Blessings of Adultery

Adultery suited me. I liked having a secret life. Racing down California freeways, bare toes gripping the accelerator, fog racing over the hills west of the Crystal Springs Reservoir and east of Half Moon Bay. The same drive that would take me to the hospital years later in the middle of the night as I followed Lueza in the ambulance. Past the wooden Episcopal church that I would choose for the funeral eight years later.

Driving away from clutter and failure and brain damage and bickering. His feet would also be bare. Enormous tanned flat feet stepping between tomato plants in his backyard garden. Putting stakes in the dirt because everything grew so high. Mexican sage and cosmos and a swollen low-lying Meyer lemon tree that gave hundreds of fruits every year. His small 1930s cottage that someone would demolish someday reeked of garlic and wood smoke from the fires he burned all winter and the salads he made most evenings. He was proud of his fire-making skills. I watched as he sliced through oak and cherry logs for the kindling basket. The relaxed muscle-memory task of dropping the axe into his latest delivery of winter wood. I stared at his hands and wrists. They could build decks and carry the disabled. It was the kind of love infatuation that was a physical sensation behind my breastbone. A beating heart that seemed much too fast and woke me up before the alarm and made me write haiku. Maybe it was hypomania, but I told myself that this ecstatic joy might make me a better person. Better to die happy. A thoughtful adulteress. A responsible cheater. Maybe we would all live longer.

After I fell in love with the fatherly boyfriend there were no more twice-a-year conjugal visits with my husband. On good days I decided that our marriage was the love of an old married couple. We still slept on our sides with his arm over my left shoulder, and there was gentle hand clasping. When the heat surges of menopause woke me, I would request arm removal and he would retreat to the far side of the king-sized mattress and snoring would begin. I watched him sleep in his Smurfy little night cap that kept his bald scalp warm. I watched and listened as his lips poofed out with each exhalation.

I was supposed to want a divorce, but life was unimaginable without him. I would miss him too much. He was my family. His family was my family. He fixed the televisions. He bought printers. He stayed on the phone for hours with technical support when it all looked hopeless. He made me tea when I was sick. I took the old-fashioned view of marriage. Land was kept together and the woman was safe to raise her children with smooth running computers. If you were very lucky you would like your husband and laugh at the same jokes. Having sex with that same person felt like incest at this point. It was unthinkable. The only love that seemed real to me was the love of children. Or love between friends. Children were the bliss. It was sometimes like living with the mentally ill, but it felt like real life. Romantic love was earth-shattering but temporary. I only wanted to be a mother and an actor. I knew my husband suffered. I knew he couldn't live like this.

Slovenian Houses

I was looking at Slovenian houses on the internet. I was reading about the wines of Italy and how they related to French wines. Watching YouTube videos of the Indonesian tsunami sweeping everything away. I wanted to know what a persimmon pudding was. And how did the electoral college really work. There were trips to Mongolia and living in yurts. Jewish funeral rituals and burial societies. The story of coffee and how it was discovered in the desert by a goatherd. I googled photographs of Japanese shrines. A website of exquisite handmade rosaries. Places to learn about the natural death movement and home funerals. There were images of tea and wooden houses in the mountains of Poland. The website about life expectancy in children who were brain damaged and physically disabled. Maybe I could rent a tiny room in an ancient house in the Dordogne. Get to know the baker and eat French peaches all summer. Mongolia still had wild places and horses to ride. Perhaps Rolfing was the answer.

I dreamed of life without clutter. Imagined rows of baskets holding gently folded sheets that had been rinsed with lavender water. Labels on everything.

Drawers full of supplies. Tape and scissors and paper clips and pens and postage stamps, batteries and glue and rubber stamps with ink pads. Ribbons and paper for wrapping gifts. Beads and string. Jars of white buttons and baskets of thread. I loved rosaries. Prayer beads. Late at night I would google *rosary* and read about its history. I imagined tea parties. Plates covered in yellow cakes and *buns.* Treats and dainties. Buns had nothing to do with hamburgers. I thought of starting a phone-tea company. Instead of phone sex, there would be conversations about tea. Darjeeling and Nepalese black. The smoky Russian teas for samovars. Teapots. Cambric tea and red-lipped children in nurseries speaking in English accents with powdered nannies who would live with them forever.

It Is What It Is and It Only Gets Worse

I almost never dreamed about Lueza. Weeks before she was born, I had a nightmare that I couldn't find her and ran through the house screaming. When she was in intensive care after her birth and we were sleeping at my parents' apartment, I dreamed that her eyes were bulging out of her head and she was dying. When she was seven, I dreamed she was lying face up, submerged in a bathtub, and I grabbed her out before she died.

I never dreamed that she could walk or talk or sit or hold her head up. I dreamed about the other crippled children doing miraculous things. Suddenly hearing a friend's child, who could only howl for vocal communication, making words and taking steps. I could never imagine Lueza being different. I couldn't picture her sitting without the support of her wheelchair and seatbelt and side supports and headrest that cradled her neck and head because she was unable to hold her body in any position. I knew so many severely disabled kids, but I would still marvel at how Lueza's physical situation was one of the worst. Her body was a combination of extreme floppiness and extreme spasticity. When you read about cerebral palsy it is always described as a *non-progressive lesion of the brain. It doesn't get better but it doesn't get worse.* I am glad that I didn't know this was a lie. It gets worse and worse. Spines become deformed. The dreaded twisting movements of dystonia. Lungs become delicate because the swallowing muscles are weak and saliva and micro-aspirations of food cause pneumonia. Aspiration pneumonia. Brain damage isn't good for swallowing.

Lueza couldn't hold up her head or her trunk, and the muscles in her arms and legs were as tight as metal cables. One year when I took her for her yearly visit to the orthopedist and showed him how bad the spine was twisting, he referred me to the other doctor in the practice whose specialty was straightening spines.

A couple of weeks later I was lifting her out of the wheelchair and placing her on the paper-covered examination table. The doctor's fingers were long and tapered, and he was explaining how my daughter should have steel rods and screws inserted along her spine to straighten it. During the procedure, the child would be cut open in the front and back, and I just kept staring at his long fingers. I made my voice high and submissive.

—I don't think we can do this with Lueza. We would be too scared to put her body through this.

—When children aren't cognitively intact we just let nature take its course. But she . . . he paused . . .

She's great. She could last a long time!

    —Oh. Thank you so much. I don't think we'll be able to do it. She's very happy and she's not in pain. She loves life. Thank you.

Burying the Dog

My husband's girlfriend's dog was dying of cancer. This was the first dog that Dora had known and loved. We had lived with this dog when the girlfriend traveled. She was old, and this was going to be her last summer. She was a large, rangy, mixed breed bitch who had been a rescue when she was a puppy. Brown body with a black face. She was probably part German shepherd and part Labrador and parts unknown. She was beloved by Sylwia and my husband and Dora.

The final crisis came on a Monday morning in the middle of summer. Marek had phoned Sylwia. It had been a bad night for the dog. She was suffering too much, and Sylwia had decided it was time to end it with the help of a vet who made home visits. A traveling Dr. Death for pets. It was decided that they would all go over and be together one last time. I wondered if we should shield Dora from this death, but I didn't want Brownie to just disappear without her saying good-bye, so we discussed it with her and a playdate was canceled and off we went to the apartment in Berkeley.

Brownie was lying on her dog bed by the windows in the living room. She looked serene. We sat on the floor in a semicircle around her and stroked her head and praised her. Dora buried her face in Brownie's neck fur. Brave and grieving. Everything in that living room felt sacred. Extreme sadness and extreme love. I felt alive.

We waited for the vet to arrive. Sylwia spoke softly to Brownie in Polish. I recognized a few of the Polish words and imagined she was telling her how beautiful and strong she was.

I saw the old station wagon pull up and park and knew that he was our doctor. There was a dog sitting next to him. I watched him collecting his bag and opening the window for the dog, and I waited at the front door so he wouldn't have to use the buzzer. I led him into the living room as if it were my home. I thanked him for making a house call. He put down his doctor bag and began assembling the tools of his trade. We probably discussed that this was the right thing to do and that Brownie had suffered enough and would not get better. He explained that it was a two-part process. One drug would put her to sleep and the other drug would stop her heart from beating. He used the electric dog clippers and shaved a small part of Brownie's leg to ready it for the injections. I tried to be calming by talking quietly to Dora about the buzzing sound of the shaver and how it wouldn't hurt Brownie. I remember sliding a Mexican blanket under the dog to absorb the urine that would leak. The blanket would double as a shroud for the burial.

And then it was over.

The thing about dead dogs is that they still look beautiful. They are covered in fur, so you don't notice that their oxygen has stopped circulating. Unlike humans, they really do look like they're sleeping.

The doctor asked if we needed help carrying Brownie into the backyard. Sylwia had injured her back while carrying her first dog in his old age, and my husband had chronic spinal pain, so I carried her body with him and thanked the doctor for his kindness. There was more kissing and stroking of Brownie, and then we wrapped her in the blanket, curled her on her side, and carried her out the back door into Sylwia's yard, where a friend had already started to dig the grave. I felt odd and serene as I lowered the blanket-wrapped dog into the ground. I was part of the ancient ritual of burial. The only other time I was able to participate in this task was when Leah, our friend's daughter at Lueza's school, had died suddenly after her eleventh birthday. It was a Jewish funeral for non-practicing Jews, and the Rabbi had told us that it was considered a blessing, a mitzvah, to help bury the deceased. There was a shovel in the pile of fresh dirt, and we each shoveled some earth over the small coffin after it was lowered into the grave.

Brownie's grave was dug by hand in this lush Berkeley backyard. Many hands and a large shovel. There was much smashing and cutting of roots to allow for the grave to be deep enough. Flowers were gathered for the bottom. Sylwia chose a dog toy to go with Brownie on her journey. She removed Brownie's leather collar. We ended with many small glasses of a sweet Polish brandy. There must have been toasting.

I don't want to be buried. I want to be burned. I don't like the idea of my bones rotting underground, and there is also the space issue. It takes too much space. I want to disappear from the Earth, although I do like the idea of having my cremains (I had learned this word from extensive research on death and dying and disposition of bodies) buried so that there will be a small spot that is marked with my life.

My husband likes the idea of natural cremation. He toured a graveyard in New Orleans on one of his business trips and was told that because New Orleans is virtually underwater people are buried in vaults above the ground, and the heat and humidity burn them up without fire. I read that in Sweden there is a company that will turn your remains into fertilizer. The process is a freeze drying and pulverizing of the body. Too much trouble. Too many steps. Tibetan sky burial is another option. You are taken to the top of a mountain in Tibet, where a special man, the bardo man, cuts your body up into little pieces and smashes it into a jelly and then flings the pieces onto rocks where birds feast on it. Nothing is wasted.

Crone Time

It was clear. Menopause was coming. The writing was on the wall. I still had my periods every month, but there was a desperation in their heaviness. I could barely leave the house. The car seat was like a crime scene. No protection was sufficient. It was as if they knew it was their last hurrah. From my research on the end of ovulation I learned that menopause was one particular day. It was the day that marked the moment of one year after the last bleeding. It was not the rest of your life.

Three stages of a woman's life: pre-fertility, fertility, and post-fertility. At either end was nonexistence. I had waited so long to have children that I was still raising them in my post-fertility days.

As they became fertile, I was entering the crone stage.

The Accidental Thanatologist

When had I become a death maven? I'd been reading the *New York Times* obituaries as long as I could remember. The clippings were in scrapbooks around my apartment. A mix of family and friends. The worst obituary was an actress friend who had died of AIDS in 1990 when she was thirty-five. My favorite was the wealthy Pittsburgh heir. The Mellon man. He took his money and left Pittsburgh and the family fortune and moved west to Arizona to begin ranching. After reading a biography of Albert Schweitzer's medical missionary work in Africa, he decided that he needed to go to medical school so that he could follow a similar path. His wife studied to become a lab technician and scrub nurse, and together they searched for the poorest place in need of help and moved to Haiti to open a hospital.

At the most recent funerals I had attended, the coffin hadn't even been lowered into the ground before we were asked to leave by the black-suited, professionally somber men. Very kindly told that it was over. The coffin lay on Astroturf, and the grave was hidden from full view. If you scanned the cemetery you could see a little dump truck patiently waiting. Lowering coffins into the earth while the family was there was not done. The exception to this was Leah, who was buried with Jewish rituals. Shoveling dirt by family and friends onto the small pine coffin was part of the ceremony. The Orthodox Jews knew what to do with a dead body. How many of my father's ancestors had been buried like this? There was no embalming or pretending that the body was just sleeping. It was considered a desecration. It was fakery. The coffin had to be unfinished pine. Closed with wooden pegs. No metal nails. The Orthodox Jews had a burial society. The body rinsed with rainwater. It was believed that the soul was hovering near. To make it less awkward, only men prepared men. Women prepared women. The genitals of the dead were always covered during preparation. Nothing was passed over the body as it was washed and dried. I felt called to this work, but as a half-Episcopalian who loved Christmas, I let it go.

I knew that I didn't want my daughter to go under the earth. I knew that I would constantly wonder what was happening to her body for years to come. There could be no rotting. I could not tolerate decomposition. If you didn't bury, then you were spared having to shop for a burial plot. There was no rush. Cremation allowed you to wait or do nothing with the remains. We could secretly fling them around her favorite rides at Disneyland. We could ride the Matterhorn and scatter a handful of dusty bones inside the mountain. It was Lueza's first rollercoaster and she had been ecstatic. My hope was that we would place the ashes in a lot of different places. I wanted some of the bone powder to be with her Polish grandfather in Warsaw. It was a family grave, and many generations were stacked inside. Lu had never traveled to Poland because that kind of trip was not an option for us. I knew families with kids in diapers and wheelchairs who flew around the country for vacations, but I couldn't imagine it. Before Lueza got her feeding tube, all food needed to be blended into a purée consistency. She couldn't drink liquids unless they were thickened with a special powder into pudding consistency; otherwise she risked choking and aspirating the fluid into her lungs. Feeding was endless. Hydration was always an issue. Places for diaper changes always needed to be found. Back seats in cars or bathroom floors. Traveling as a family was only possible in our wheelchair van, and I dreaded those trips. Lueza was not happy in cars or vans. When we lived in New York City she would shriek during taxi rides. In our California life she rode in her wheelchair in the center of the van, but she never slept and, once, to keep her happy and not screaming, we played "When You Walk through a Storm" from *Carousel* fifty times. Dora was in the back seat behind her sister's wheelchair training a tiny robotic dog to sit.

What would Dora remember from this life with her sister? I would remember so much joy. The screaming at night and Lu's intermittent extreme insomnia and my terror of what was coming were drifting to the side of my memory, and the joyful part of it was all I wanted to see. The truth is that Lulu woke up smiling every day of her life. One of my favorite photos is the moment after waking up from her tracheotomy. She was peaceful. Calm abiding. A slightly amused serenity. Unaware or uninterested in the little plastic tube emerging from her neck. Tubes had saved her again. A feeding tube. Now a breathing tube. I was euphoric.

When my Jewish grandfather was buried, we left the graveside before the coffin was placed in the ground. When my Episcopalian grandfather died I don't remember anything being done. Maybe he was cremated straight from the hospital, where he lay motionless after a massive stroke. I can't remember. I remember my Episcopalian grandmother's feet when she was dying. I had stopped by my parents' apartment moments after Grandma had collapsed on her way back to her bedroom in the back hallway. Stopped by to say hello on the way back to my roommates in the West Side apartment. I yodeled down the hallway to see who was home. Mother ran toward me.

—Hurry, Granny is dying.

Resting in bed one moment and then the bathroom visit and sudden collapse. The home health aide and my mother had gotten her back into bed as she began what is called *active dying*. The nurse kept lifting the blanket to look at the color of her feet. I found it intrusive but said nothing. I held my grandmother's hand and wondered how long this dying would last. I now knew what the dreaded death rattle was. The sound of air going through a throat that was wet and collapsing. I told Granny that I loved her. She wished me well with my work in theater. She knew she was leaving us. When she saw the family doctor arrive, she asked him how he was. She didn't ask anyone to save her. And then the well-wishing was over and she went into the intense business of dying a natural death. My father waited with the doctor in the hallway outside her bedroom. The final dying took about half an hour. She would take one long hard breath, which seemed like the last one until twenty seconds later when she would breathe again. It sounded like suffocating. She couldn't speak anymore, she could only breathe. Grandma wanted a quiet death without rescue. We needed to let her die. Her fingers in my hand. Wanting this to end. Watching my first death. Sweet, powdery-smelling grandmother. And it ended.

My mother phoned the minister from the Episcopal church around the corner. He came thirty minutes later to help with the details. Who to call for *removal of the body*. Grandma was a body now. She had to leave home with strangers. I remember the gurney with a red canvas zip-up body bag on top. That's how Grandma left her room in my parents' apartment. They rolled her past us and into the front elevator. What if people were in the lobby coming home from a fancy party when Grandma was leaving? Would they ask the doorman who was going? Maybe that would be considered rude and they would only speak in whispers once they got into the elevator and were alone. Would their evening be ruined? Would they have an extra drink upstairs and look out at the Metropolitan Museum of Art and across the reservoir to Central Park West and know that it was probably that little old woman who lived in the maid's room of her daughter's apartment? She walked with a cane and always wore suede Tretorn sneakers because nothing else was comfortable after her "feet went all funny." Toes twisting over to the side and thickened nails that would require a sander for grooming. The building was a co-op, so they probably had a rule book that explained proper procedures for removing a dead body. I didn't know it then, but I should've gone with her. I didn't know.

Nobody should go alone with strangers to a crematorium.

Hospital World

The siege of the summer of 2008. Fifty-four days in the hospital. From Three North to Three South to PICU and back again. Three West with the transplant kids and then back to the other wing with kids fighting constant seizures or out of control neurological states. When I wasn't talking with a doctor or suctioning secretions out of Lueza's throat, I was on my laptop looking up Buddhist death rituals or eyebrow restoration or white kitchens with open shelves. I wrote prayers in the big leather book of the tiny meditation sanctuary room near the death and dying of the PICU and the NICU. The book was for parents who were sitting vigil. It was the summer of acronyms. On really bad days I threw the I Ching and did single-card readings of a Tarot deck. The I Ching spoke of transformation, and the Tarot cards were about despair and death.

I loved the hospital. Lu loved the hospital. She loved the attention. There was always someone to watch. Or friends were visiting. The wandering bands of young resident doctors. The whirring machines, suction catheters attached to beds, oxygen, the beeping, people awake all night working just outside your room. It had the constant noise and uneasy peace of a night flight across the Atlantic Ocean. You were never alone. You could wander out of your child's hospital room at three a.m. and there was someone sitting quietly at a desk working on a computer, and they would answer your question or help you deal with a new catastrophic antibiotic-induced diarrhea. During the day I would leave the door open so I could see everyone as they walked by. Our favorite resident might visit us. Doctors in pediatric residency were learning from Lueza. They would ask me about the decisions that we were facing and what was important. One morning I heard the sound of classical guitar music and opened the door to a bearded man sitting in the hall outside of Lulu's room playing Bach. There was a pain-management golden retriever that worked with a nurse and visited children who were undergoing painful procedures. A beautiful gray-haired chaplain would check on us. We would stand in the hall, and she would listen to me talk about Lueza and how I had been living with the idea of approaching death for so long. There was great coffee in the basement cafeteria and more doctors in scrubs with kind faces who weren't surprised when they saw me back at the hospital for the fourth time in five months. Nurses now referred to Lueza as a *frequent flyer*.

I felt safe. I could escape my identity as a Neurotic and become a Strong Mother of a Gravely Ill Child. The helicopter was always landing on the roof for the most recent emergency transport. Children were wheeled around in little red wagons instead of wheelchairs. Older children with hairless chemo heads sat in the lounge tethered to IV poles and computer screens. The parents wandered around dazed and weighed down with the rest of the family and bags of food that they consumed in their hospital rooms. In the wing where Lulu always ended up, there were rooms with two hospital beds and two built-in Naugahyde-covered sleeping couch–beds for parents. If you were lucky, they thought your child might be contagious and you got a single room. The ceiling was fitted with tracks for a series of bright-colored curtains to give each family a little imaginary privacy. I always listened in when the doctors stopped by to consult with the current roommate. I had been told by another mother of a child with disabilities that if your child was in PICU there were no beds for adults and parents would stake out areas of the hallway for sleeping. There were conference areas that would turn into bunk rooms at night. PICU was behind two large swinging doors. Many children were on ventilators. Parents were crazed. If you fell asleep, you were woken and told there was no sleeping in PICU. I had never been there but imagined it to be like the NICU where Lueza had started her life. The *No Exit* of the hospital world.

This was Lueza's fourth hospital stay and second 911 call. I can't remember if this was the third or fourth pneumonia. The dreaded aspiration pneumonia. When food or fluid is inhaled into the lungs. Common with severely disabled children with weak swallowing muscles and no head control. She had been feverish for a couple of days on Fourth of July weekend and we were going to take her to the pediatrician on Monday. On Sunday I had driven Dora and her best friend to their first sleepaway camp. A five-hundred-mile roundtrip drive to the Sierras with the air cloudy from summer forest fires. I stopped in a roasting hot Truckee to take a walk and drink a sad root beer float before the long drive west on 80. Many tourists wandered through bead stores and ice cream shops and shellacked redwood table stores. The recurring image of the drive home was swollen dead deer on the side of the road with stiff cartoon legs in the air. I was in a fugue state of dread.

At home, Lueza was hot with fever. Doctor appointments were scheduled for the following morning. No point to spend all night awake in the ER, we told ourselves.

At eight a.m. she was in respiratory distress. Almost silent. Barely breathing. I screamed for Marek to call 911. Minutes later, barking Daisy closed in bedroom, sirens blaring, paramedics entered our house with big black briefcases of life-saving equipment; nebulizers poured mist into her airway, stabilized her, and we were back at our hospital within twenty-five minutes without a siren.

The summer of love. Friends roaring down freeways to hug us and hold Lu and suggest the newest biopharma lung drug. The summer of survival. The summer of the codes. Rapid response and code blue and saving her life with the big blue rubber squeeze ball that pumped air into her lungs until she could breathe. A nasal trumpet got her breathing when my husband and I were kicked out of the room during a code blue on Bastille Day. The summer of the respiratory therapists. Respiratory therapists save people. They can open a blocked trachea during a code blue. The airway is their world. How to keep a human breathing.

This was the summer of BiPAP. Bi-level positive airway pressure. People with obstructive sleep apnea or children with collapsing airways used the same device. A mask strapped to the face attached to a machine that blows the air in with such pressure that the airway can't collapse. I tried it on, and it was like sticking your face out of the window of a speeding car. The sleep apnea crowd just strapped it on at bedtime, but Lu was hooked up as soon as she arrived in the emergency room that morning, and every time they tried to remove it her airway would collapse.

So this was the conversation that was hanging over the hospital summer. The conversation was a big question. If Lueza cannot breathe without a BiPAP machine attached to her face, then how will she ever get out of the hospital? And, more importantly, how will she ever breathe on her own?

And this was where her favorite pulmonologist, Dr. Robinson, raised the subject of a tracheotomy. I was driving when I first heard him say the word.

Tracheotomy.

And I stopped breathing.

I didn't know where we were anymore.

And while you and your husband and the doctors are trying to figure out the best way forward for Lueza, after conferences with doctors and phone calls with other parents and long nights of Google research, on a Saturday morning at Lucile Packard Children's Hospital, your thirteen-year-old daughter goes into respiratory distress and a code blue is called and the doctors from the PICU rush in to assess and you are calmly asked by the head doctor if you want your daughter intubated. You are given the option to let her die by suffocation. And you don't scream at this doctor. You hold your daughter's tiny peony-soft feet and calm yourself by feeling the pads of her toes because your daughter is beyond consciousness and you reply: Yes please.

And the beautiful Indian doctor with the name of a goddess, who asked if you wanted your daughter to be saved, instructs the pediatric resident about sedation and intubation, the insertion of a tube connected to oxygen down her trachea, and it is done.

Lueza went from dying of suffocation to deeply asleep and serene.

I had gone from a catatonic shock to wild joy.
Lueza showed them what she needed.
Time to sign up for the dreaded tracheotomy.

Hoping for Pancakes

I have always liked being unconscious. I think I love sleep too much. Sleep without dreams is preferable. My dreams are exhausting. Once upon a time I wrote them down in a small notebook, but now the notebook is in a box somewhere in the garage with my gallstones. An undisciplined woman. There are some basic themes of catastrophic dream images. Being surrounded by rattlesnakes. Tornados heading straight for me. Terrorists slaughtering people. An unusually high tide rushing toward me. Ceilings bowed and blistered with flooding water from above. Speeding into traffic the wrong way. Seeing airplanes crashing. Being in an airplane that is flying under bridges. Clogged toilets. And insomnia is always lurking.

I had left Lulu in the hospital with Marek for the second night of what we were calling the third pneumonia so that I could spend the night with Dora before her three-day science camp in the redwoods. I wanted to do something special with her because I had spent so much time in the hospital since late December, and Dora was constantly getting dropped off with friends and doing extra sleepovers and pretending that it was all fine. I was planning to let Dora sleep with me the night before the trip and then to send her off with a big pancake breakfast. Whole-wheat pancakes made from scratch, I announced to anyone who would listen. I had stopped using mixes or measurements and just poured whole-wheat flour, baking powder, eggs, melted butter, and milk into a bowl. When Lulu was eating by mouth she could devour four giant pancakes puréed with milk and real maple syrup in the tiny food processor.

After Dora was packed and curled on her side in my bed, I mixed up the batter and left it in the fridge. I was an organized happy mother. I almost didn't notice the tiny brown bottle of liquid lorazepam. It was a just-in-case medication for Lu when she left the hospital the first time. We were instructed to give her a dose only if she was extremely agitated at night and couldn't sleep. We had used it a few times and the bottle looked empty. I held up the dark brown glass to the light to make sure there was nothing left. We had been through so many bad nights of screaming and writhing with no medical help, and now we had good drugs. Before dropping it in the recycle bag, I thought that a couple of drops of lorazepam might help me sleep, and I tipped my head back and let it drip onto my tongue. It felt oily and tasted like poison. I headed to my computer for the night's news reading and googling of medical information. Third pneumonia in a couple of months. Death and dying. Home funerals.

My mind was racing, and I hoped the bitter drops would deliver sleep.

After about twenty-two minutes of internet reading on homemade burial shrouds and expensive wool blankets from an island in Maine with special sheep, I started to feel the relaxation of the drug and closed up my laptop to crawl into bed with Dora.

I must have set the alarm on my phone to wake us up for the wonderful pancake breakfast and sendoff, but I can't remember anything but Dora yelling about how late it was and how she had to get to school and I was still in bed. I almost fell down the stairs to the front hall from sudden vertigo and turned around to rush to the toilet for immediate vomiting. I remember telling Dora that I couldn't drive and that she should call the friends who lived nearby and they could pick her up and get her to school in time for the bus ride to the camp in the redwood forest. There would be no pancakes.

Wicked Mommy

Her lip started to lift up and away from her top teeth as the nasolabial folds creased, hands on her steering wheel in the parking lot of Dora's school. I could smell her skin. She thought I was making a bad decision and pulled up the muscles of her upper eyelids to show fear.

I told her I was going on tour with the musical *Wicked*.

—But it's all in the west. It starts in Southern California and then Fresno and I'll be able to come home every two or three weeks for three days.

Probably every three weeks, and I'll get personal days for Dora's eighth-grade graduation, and if Lueza gets sick I'll be a car ride or a quick flight away, and Marek will be working from home, and it's a lot of money, and I can't wait at home and never leave because I'm afraid for Lueza, was going through my head.

I left on March 17, 2011, and drove to Costa Mesa to join the Munchkinland Tour. Before I left, I took Lu to see her favorite pulmonary doctor because she had another fever and we needed to get her chest x-rayed and make sure she didn't need to be admitted to the hospital again.

Dr. Robinson gave us good news. No hospital. Just another round of ciprofloxacin and no school. She would be fine.

I would see them all in less than three weeks.

She May Be Lying Down but She May Be Very Happy

When Lueza was about eleven months old and could not lift her head or roll over or pick up a toy, I looked at my husband as if I might start screaming and asked him: Will she always be LYING DOWN?

He is an interpreter. He can speak and write in Polish and Russian and English. He understands language. He knew I was asking if the horror was happening and, if it was, how would we survive knowing that our daughter was injured beyond repair.

How would I not go insane?

He said: She may be lying down, but she may be very happy.

Here's the thing. We had been on a journey of accepting the unacceptable since the hour of her birth. We thought she would die that first night, and then I thought I would die from the anguish of what she had lost and suffered through, but we were born into a new life and there was joy again because Lueza loved this life.

She may be lying down, but she may be very happy.

Yes she had the misery of frustration when she couldn't get us to understand what it was she wanted to watch or listen to or what story she wanted us to tell, but she loved Dora and us and her caregivers and her teachers at school. She loved her grandparents and her two uncles and one aunt. When she was in the emergency room at three in the morning, she wasn't frightened, because the male nurse who was taking care of her was handsome and she was grinning and flirting and she was not like me. She was not afraid. There was always singing and movies and we would hold her in our arms and dance.

Lueza loved rollercoasters and the Matterhorn at Disneyland. She flew through a dark fake Swiss–Italian mountain in our laps and laughed until the ride stopped. She loved the Jurassic Park ride at Universal Studios. Sitting in a large open boat that falls down a waterfall as I held her chest and head with my arm and braced her into the seat with my left leg over her lap. She became obsessed with the ride called Back to the Future at Universal Studios. We carried her in our arms into the pretend DeLorean car and flew into space five times in a row. Marek always planned the trips to Universal Studios with all of us riding in the wheelchair van.

Lueza liked when we swung her in the green

cotton blanket back and forth over her futon. Lueza loved when Dora got mad and cried. She loved movie musicals. She watched Robert Goulet on YouTube. Gordon MacRae. She loved Julie Andrews. Rodgers and Hammerstein. Sondheim's *Pacific Overtures* and *Into the Woods* and *Sunday in the Park With George*. *Carousel* and *The Sound of Music* and *Cinderella*. Lueza loved handsome men.

The Phone Call that Comes

Lueza died in her bed at dawn. She was sick again. Coughing and fever. She wouldn't smile at me on Skype on the Saturday or was it Sunday? I did all my tricks. I said Polish swear words. I did my ridiculous dialects. She didn't respond to any of it. I was happy I would drive home the next day and be with her. I had a bad feeling.

I took a sleeping pill the night she died. The doctors had told my husband not to bring Lueza to the emergency room. There were too many sick children, and she was too vulnerable. Much better to wait and see her doctors in the morning. No reason to be up all night in the ER waiting to get admitted. Much better for Lulu to be at home with Daddy and Dora. They all agreed. I agreed. She always slept alone with her oxygen monitor taped around her second toe and the misting machine blowing cool moist air into her tracheotomy tube on her neck. The red oxygen light on her toe. Calming white noise of the machine giving her extra oxygen while she slept. She was always fine at night.

I was four hundred miles away. The next day I would drive home.

I'd just finished my first week of performances with the *Wicked* tour. I performed my last show of the first week on tour and sipped wine with a new friend in my dressing room in Costa Mesa before going back to the hotel and packing for the drive home the next morning. The stage fright had been shocking at first. I was sure it was time to stop performing onstage. How could I get up in front of two thousand people and not feel like dying? I was outside my body. I was turning to anyone standing backstage before my entrance and telling them how terrified I was. I would need to quit this business.

Two days later, it was gone. I felt the joy of disappearing into this crazy narcissistic weather sorceress Madame Morrible. Rhymes with horrible. This lover of thaumaturgy. This caster of spells. The only evil character in the show. The Kabuki-like mask of my makeup and costumes. The young company welcoming and embracing me. I thought I could tour and make money and come home every two weeks. I had snuck away from home one afternoon to drive south. Daddy would keep everything together.

The cell phone was vibrating next to my head. Husband sounded strange. Was he breathing funny? I probably said: WHAT? His words: Lueza died. I opened my throat and screamed. I stopped and did it again. Two shrieks at eight a.m. on April 4, 2011, at the Marriott in Costa Mesa, California. I called the hotel lobby.

—Please help me, my daughter just died.

They came upstairs and sat with me and asked what they could do. There was nothing they could do but sit with me for a few moments, and then I knew. The only possibility. I called my production stage manager. I called David. A stage manager is a crisis manager. He keeps a show running no matter what disaster occurs. He fields all the calls of who is sick on any given day and who will substitute for that actor. He gets understudies onstage in the middle of a show when an actor starts vomiting or a vocal cord stops phonating. He keeps actors safe from moving set pieces that may malfunction or crush them. He is the one who decides when the curtain comes down if an audience member collapses and the show must stop while people are carried up aisles to the rescuers. David packed me up and took control of my car. He drove me to an airport and walked me to security. Understudies would take over. Producers would be called.

I had been studying death rituals for years. When Lueza was living at the hospital, I asked the chaplain what happened to children who died. How did they get them out of hospital rooms past all the other worried parents who were sitting vigil? How did they get them past the happy visitors with Mylar balloons for the new mothers who were right down the hall from the sickest children in the hospital? You couldn't have dead children being wheeled past parents. How did they sneak them out? The chaplain explained that hospital beds had movable sides that could rise and obscure what they carried and back halls were very handy.

But Lulu died at home. She was ours. No professionals.

Henry picked me up at the airport. He had already picked up my husband's girlfriend at the BART station and delivered her to our home.

I couldn't run into the house screaming for Lulu. Dora was standing in the kitchen. Waiting for Mommy. I needed to comfort and hold her before walking the ten steps into the little bedroom off the kitchen where Lueza lay. Did I fall to the floor when I saw her? I can't remember. Lulu's eyes were open. I tried to close them like I had seen in movies, but it didn't work. I covered her in kisses. I probably wept. I felt my daughter's body. How could I distinguish the difference between Lulu's spasticity and the rigidity that death brings?

I called the Episcopal priest from Dora's school. I wanted bedside prayers. He would have holy water. The Episcopal priest would come to our home, and we would surround her with love and prayers. A death at home. No screaming sirens and paramedics to frighten her at the end.

After the minister left, I knew the plan from years of reading about handling a death at home. Lulu needed to be moved out of her room that faced the afternoon sun. She needed the cool room that was always shaded and ground level with a sliding glass door. My husband and his girlfriend and my big boyfriend and I gathered around Lulu's futon and took corners and edges of the pale green cotton blanket and lifted her off the mattress. This was the swinging blanket when she was smaller. She was so tiny and she loved the movement. Lu's room opened onto the deck with a sliding glass door. We stepped outside onto the redwood deck that we had built for her wheelchair entrance; workmen in the neighbor's backyard saw us and smiled and waved a big hello. Maybe they thought we were moving furniture on that blanket. The fence was high. The deck was higher. We smiled and waved. The room downstairs was an extra room. Lu's caregiver had stripped the bed and remade it with a layer of diaper pads held tight by a fitted sheet. Dora put flowers on the bed. Early April in Northern California and everything was erupting. Lavender from the bush in the front yard and apple and pear blossoms. Calla lilies emerged like weeds. Orange blossom–perfumed day.

When I called our precinct to report Lueza's death, they informed me that the protocol was to send the fire truck with the paramedics. Sirens down the street again. Locking the dogs in a room. Paramedics surrounding her flowery death bed. EKG wires had to be attached to Lueza's chest. Brief compressions were done for a paper printout of the flatline. Me explaining about all the middle-of-the-night deaths with these delicate children. These children die, I explained. This is our life, I told them.

I understood their situation. As soon as they spoke with Lueza's pulmonologist, they packed their black cases and left.

My parents arrived from New York by evening. My father was on the kitchen computer. Mother was upstairs in our room after visiting her flower-covered granddaughter in the downstairs bedroom that used to be theirs when they visited. The house was freezing in April. My mother was always cold. We moved electric heaters into rooms when they visited. We gave them metal pods that you filled with hot water and buried under sheets. I helped her into warm socks. Her feet were a completely different shape from before. The toes were longer. They were canted at an angle. The toenails were curved and the nail beds were humped up. Did all feet change? Was it arthritis? I wondered what my face looked like as I held my mother's foot and slipped it into the soft tennis socks. Was I wincing? Did I look disgusted? My mother had been the only one with beautiful feet in the family. Fine strong arches. Well-proportioned straight toes. Not sad flat feet with floppy toes and ripped nails. How could none of us have inherited her feet? Mother would have wanted us to have been comfortable in our skins.

Lueza stayed with us in the downstairs bedroom for twenty-four hours. My husband slept on the floor next to her bed. Dora and I slept on Lu's futon upstairs. The undertakers picked her up at eight a.m. on Tuesday morning. We went with her to the local funeral home. We requested the option of visitation. Three days. No embalming. Like an old-fashioned death at home. Time to spend with her in a small room with a couch and two stuffed chairs. Lulu was on a padded table covered by a coral cotton blanket. A private wake with no alcohol. She was kept cool at night and then moved to the room for our visits. We sat and held her hand. Kissed her face. There was no sobbing. One of our Filipina night nurses stopped by with her small son.

On cremation morning she was lying in her small cardboard coffin on top of the padded table. I photographed her. We brought calla lilies and lavender and orange blossoms from our front yard for the inside of her coffin. Marek asked me to shave his head right before going to the funeral home. Snippings of Dora's hair and mine and Marek's and more lavender were placed in a small muslin bag that we put next to her.

So we can find each other, my husband said.

Cursed and Covered in Salt

My house was a mess. There were piles of mail on the kitchen table. I deserved nothing. I needed to convince myself that all was not lost and I should get out of the bed. Coffee was what usually cheered me on. Just the thought of coffee. The ritual of making it. Filling the electric kettle. The unbleached paper filters and smell of fair-trade, women-picked Guatemalan coffee that waited in the recyclable brown bag. I had hope that I could persuade myself that I deserved to live. Not literally. I wasn't a suicide waiting to happen. This was suicidal ideation. Just walk off the path and fall in the woods and see if anyone finds me. Fling myself off a ridge that isn't too steep near the redwoods in Portola Valley and wait to be rescued. This was a mind-torturing exercise for me. A mental raking over the coals of my life. A psychological hair shirt. Self-laceration. Indulgent self-mutilation of the psyche. No more physical slashings with sharp objects but secret slashings against my self. I condemned myself for obsessive introspection and self-loathing. I condemned myself for condemning myself. Even my suffering was selfish. Get out of your head and do something. Do something for someone else.

If I became a hospice volunteer, would this stop? If I did loving-kindness meditation, could I convince myself to be kind? I thought of moving to Africa and living in an orphanage. I thought of living in my bed.

Life in a graveyard. Everything had disappeared. My daughter had died in her bed, and the room was hallowed ground. Before the sudden death, Dora had decided to move 2,800 miles away for a boarding high school in Connecticut. The empty nest was sudden and shocking. Ground zero. There was no sound of a movie musical playing or oxygen machine mechanically puffing. Lueza's room was a shrine. Her ashes were there. Her music. Drawers of polar fleece jackets and plastic-wrapped unworn sweaters. A row of footwear. Tiny Converse sneakers. Mushroomy tiny brown sheepskin-lined boots because her feet were always cold. Blue and brown leather open-toed sandals for hot weather. Wheelchair shoes. The tiny shoes looked new because her feet never touched the ground.

Treasures were everywhere. Tiny nail clippers. The body oil from the last Christmas that was used every Sunday by our beloved Bosnian part-time caregiver, whom we found through a newspaper ad that I placed in the local free paper. She would warm up the room with the space heater and position Lulu with pillows, naked and diapered, and massage her spastic muscles while they watched *Carousel, Mary Poppins,* or *Hairspray*. The last batch of birthday cards were taped to the bookshelf next to her bed so she could look at the glitter-glue pink and green Little Mermaid wishing her a happy sixteenth birthday. Salmon-colored diapers for children weighing over fifty pounds. Sacred-memory diapers. Never to be thrown away. I will be buried with all of this. I didn't believe in cleaning out the room and getting on with life. This was my life. I needed to figure out how to live without her the way we figured out how to live when she was so severely injured on the day of her birth.

Was this toxic grief? What was the word for when your grief was bad? Grief that went on for too long and was wrong. Pathological grief? Shitty grief? I had my happy memories and my photos and I had my grief. I attended a grief group for parents whose children had died. Suicides and drug overdoses and car accidents and cancer and drowning. We read a credo before the meeting started. Candles were lit, and we shared stories and books, and people wept and hugged, and I felt love for these humans. I held strangers and told them about Lueza's death and why I wouldn't clean out her room. At the end of the meeting we all held hands and said goodnight to our children.

Grief experts were everywhere. Another human condition that humans had forgotten how to do. Grief coaches to assist the mediocre grievers. I did my own version. I played one of Lulu's favorite Disney songs and fell forward from my knees onto her futon and sobbed until it shifted into screaming with my face in the cotton blankets and homemade quilts given to us by neighbors as blood vessels burst under my eyes, and I would shower and feel stunned and walk around town wearing sunglasses.

When my father visited ten months after the death, he looked at the closed door and asked if we had switched it back into a TV room yet. I went into the sedating part of my brain, far from the amygdala, and said: No. No, we haven't done anything with the room.

Jizo

The Jizo Ceremony for Children Who Have Died was held in a yurt at the Zen Center in Marin County just north of San Francisco. The yurt is down a steep hill, a short walk from where I park my car. I smell eucalyptus tree oil and tarweed, and the breeze is cooled by Pacific fog. I have my two pieces of red fabric with needles and thread and scissors in a plastic sandwich bag. We will be making something, the website explains. Red fabric is required. An arts-and-crafts grief ceremony for children who have died and the people they left behind. A Jizo ceremony. A Japanese deity, who is depicted in statues as a baby Buddha. Sometimes Jizo is sitting with legs crossed. Sometimes standing, staff in hand, wearing a red fabric cape or hood. He is the protector of women in labor and the souls of children who have died. I am a Jewish–Episcopalian with no proper grieving rituals, and I want this time with sad parents and grandparents surrounded by organic gardens and fog and meditators in small wood houses.

At the the center of the yurt are scissors and bunches of rosemary and pens and paper. I brought a large square of red velour that I cut from a pair of Lu's leggings. I fill it with rosemary, which is supplied by our Zen guides. Rosemary is for remembrance, they say. Write prayers to your child, they say, and I add small rolled tubes of paper prayers tied with twine to the red pouch I sew together at each end.

My daughter was Lueza, I tell a group of strangers. We circle the room following the Zen priests holding our red fabric offerings to Jizo. I try to remember their children's names as we walk in a circle saying: *Gate gate paragate parasamgate bodhi svaha. (Gone, gone, gone beyond, gone all together beyond. Awakened spirit Aaaaahh!)*

Dreaming of Art

I dip the burning incense stick in the cold tea. My bedroom is too smoky. I collect the pile of burned matches and drop them into the tiny matchbox. It makes me think of tiny art. People probably create miniature worlds and insert them into these matchboxes. People who spend their lives making art. I imagine poets at their kitchen tables or in small cabins in dry woods on mountainsides. Writing every day. The discipline of a monk. The life of a disciple.

Sometimes I imagine my daughter. It's a conscious conjuring of Lueza in my mind's eye. I see an open wooden temple next to a humid green river, and there are elderly Thai monks in the temple, and one of them who is very old but strong is holding her in his arms. Her white skin in his brown arms. They are both laughing. We all go into the warm water. Lueza was unafraid of water. Rollercoasters made her laugh uncontrollably. She loved the movement. She could only feel fast movement this way. Her body was always held. In arms or in wheelchairs with straps, padded side supports, and a head rest that held up her neck and head. She went down slides on our laps when she was small. She sat on our laps to swing. Her gross motor physical development never progressed beyond the level of a three-month-old baby. She always wore diapers. She was always fed by mouth until she was thirteen, and then the tube feeding. She was never able to hold anything in her hands. Her spine pretzeled.

I would breathe her in. Smell her skin and her hair. Mash my mouth into her cheek for kisses. Help her cough by pressing a certain way on her upper ribcage or lightly clapping her back with cupped hands to use the breath to clear her airways. Live with her in hospitals. Lie next to her and watch *The Little Mermaid* and *State Fair* and *The Sound of Music* and *The Little Princess*. Watch her wake up smiling every morning. You couldn't possibly imagine that her life would be joyful, but this is how she dragged you up and into life. This was the fucking silver lining.

There Are Men in My House

There are men in my house. They are American and Mexican, Guatemalan and Irish. They are carpenters and roofers and tapers and dry-wallers, mold abatement fixers and demolition guys with gas masks for protection. They crack open the kitchen. Hack out the appliances and walls and floors. They remove asbestos. A Mexican man in painter whites hops around on stilts as he swabs the new drywall with a powdery plaster compound. Manny the sub-carpenter finds the remnants of a rats' nest under the laundry floor, and Russell discovers black mold in the attic space over the dryer. They are fixing everything.

Russell is the head carpenter and tall as a Dutchman. I do what I did in the hospital with the doctors. I want them to like me. I tell Russell about Lueza and explain that she died in the little room behind the laundry machines. It was her bedroom, I explain. I make sure he sees her photos before we remove everything prior to demolition. A larder will be born where the washing machine stood. A larder filled with homemade strawberry preserves and chutneys, pickles, and brandied cherries on one side of the hallway, and the stacked washer and dryer on the other. Lueza's room will become a home office with a desk as wide as the little room.

After the demolition, I find the wooden strip of doorway with the yearly markings of Dora's growth. There is one line for me. There is one for Marek and a few for Dora's beautiful red-haired friend Natalie, who grew and grew and always made Lueza laugh. Russell knew to save it. Now I love Russell, but not love-affair love. His height and girth makes me want to curl up in his shirt pocket and cling to his neck. He is saving my home.

Every day I get photographs from Russell showing hidden mistakes and faulty work done by the previous owner because he knew how to build things but not things that would last. The electricians find wires that shouldn't be where they are, and I tell them how we almost had a fire one night in a kitchen wall and how firemen saved us and I've always lived in fear about what is hiding in these walls that might blow up or burn us down.

Suburban archaeology. Three layers of linoleum floors are uncovered. Asbestos is revealed. Back to the 1930s. Wisps of dusty sweet potato–colored wallpaper I have never seen peek out behind destroyed walls. I peel them off and stick them between pages in a book. They will become art.

I'm nonplussed that I never heard the rats under the washing machine floor. I am always listening for rats. They stay hidden in these California suburban neighborhoods, but if you look—and I do—you can see them crawling at night, cartoon figures backlit by the neighbors' lights, across the fences that line our little lots. At dusk I see them foraging in our plum tree.

I scream when Russell tells me about the rats' nest. He shows me the indentation where they slept. I scream two more times at the thought of the nearness of rats. "I'm theatrical," I say as Manny peers down from the attic space at the high-pitched sound. I want them to laugh. I want to be a special client. Maybe they will work harder when they know that I am a kind person who is terrified of rats and has survived my daughter's death in this house.

A few days after the demolition begins in the kitchen, everything is gone. The rectangular room reminds me of the dark wooden barn in the Adirondacks where my mother grew up. The peppery smell of old wood. No interior walls. I plead with Russell to close all possible entry holes that rodents might find. The paper chaos of my kitchen desk has been relocated to clear plastic boxes in my bedroom. Lueza's medical reports are resting in sealed containers in the garage. The bag of tiny sheepskin boots and sandals are in a bag for donation. I curate another few boxes for Dora's art and essays. Her first tracings of letters. Religious drawings of Jesus and Mary from the Episcopal day school. A felt-tip marker creation of a fiery orange angel Gabriel in flight over a kneeling Mary in prayer.

They are all safe now.

I ask Russell to let me know when they are going to close up the walls in the kitchen. There will be framing, electrics will be placed, and then insulation before the drywall will seal everything. I want to place a time capsule behind the kitchen walls. A space behind the living room fireplace is revealed. Slices of wood slathered with concrete from the 1930s. Wood-and-cement-created nooks. There will be room to place a small container.

There's a tin in my bathroom stuffed with old cotton balls and extra dental floss. It is decorated with a family of fictional mice. If I could be a mouse, I would want to live with them. Books and teapots and fresh baked cakes fill their home.

I empty the tin and roam my house for photographs. Lueza and Dora on a Christmas card that I never sent. Marek and me and Lueza and Dora on a cloudy Northern California beach when Lueza was small enough for me to carry her like a baby. A photograph of Dora at her high school graduation. Photos of both dogs. I put in small gifts. A smooth chunk of rose quartz. A bracelet of wooden beads. I find the secret metal capsule that I bought in 1999 at an art supply store. The size of a vitamin capsule. It unscrews. Inside is a rolled-up scroll of blank paper. *We were so happy here,* I write. I nestle the metal capsule under the photographs.

A few days later, Russell tells me that the drywall men will be coming, and I settle the tin behind the fireplace.

The men fill my home with their lunches and their music. There are Spanish and English, Irish and American accents. Sometimes there is yelling. I hear screaming saws. My plaster dust footprints are everywhere. They look like my feet. Second toe longer than the first. Negative space for the little arches.

Strong feet.

I live here.

Home.

Birthday party at the ice-skating rink

ACKNOWLEDGMENTS

Enormous gratitude to Meghan Daum, who introduced me to Scott Parker and David Oates at Kelson Books.

Thank you to the doctors who loved Lueza and took care of her. Dr. Ed Davies and Dr. Leon Root in New York City. In California, there was Lucile Packard Children's Hospital and the pediatric residents, specialists, and hospitalists who cared for her and guided us through medical crises.

We will always be grateful for Lueza's care at LPCH. Dr. John Peoples, Dr. Michele Long, Dr. Rebecca Blankenberg, Dr. Terry Robinson, Dr. Doug Mogul, Dr. Mitchell Lunn. The respiratory therapists and the nurses and our chaplain, Carolyn Glauz-Todrank.

I want to thank my parents and siblings for their love and support in those first nine months and forever after.

Thank you to the women who helped us take care of Lueza. Vicky, Charito, Basia, Eva, Timea, Edit, Lucila, Sebiha, Vilma, Bernabeth, Ann, and Jill.

Thank you to our schools. United Cerebral Palsy, Standing Tall, Bridge School, and Avalon Academy. Thank you to the late Pegi Young and Jim Forderer and to Marilyn Buzolich for starting the Bridge School, and to Neil Young for his massive contributions to the kids. Thank you, Lynette and Kinga and Annie for the brilliant school that is Avalon.

Thank you to my teachers. Meghan Daum, Mark Matousek, Ann Randolph, Abigail Thomas, and Lidia Yuknavitch. Thank you to the writers who read earlier pages. Elizabeth Aquino, Barbara Graham, Melody Lawrence, and Martin Moran. Massive gratitude to Lisa Leguillou and Paul Dobie at Wicked.

Thank you, friends and family. Harry Brown, John Augustine, Julie Hagerty, David Hirson, Jolanta Szczęsna, Mikołaj Jarkowski, Jakub Szczęsny, Bozena Gilewska, Karen Tull, Henry Stram, Judy Blazer, and my sister Connie Gelb.

And thank you to Kirby Wilkins for showing me the way.

Jody Gelb has been an actor in New York and San Francisco for more than forty years. She has appeared on Broadway in *Wicked*, *The Who's Tommy*, *Big River*, *Titanic*, and *Wrong Mountain*. She is the author of solo shows *Past Lives* and *Does the Noise In My Head Bother You?* This is her first book.